"Black 12", a Messerschmitt Bf 109 E-3, was forced down by Spitfires near Manston on 27 November 1940. It was subsequently repaired and used for test purposes. The aircraft is now on display in the Royal Air Force Museum in Hendon.v

Messerschmitt Bf 109 E

Rudolf Höfling

I0809161

The Designer Dipl. Ing. Willy Messerschmitt

Born the son of a wine merchant in Frankfurt am Main, as a youth Willy Messerschmitt was fascinated by aviation and progressed from building flying scale models to gliders. In the summer of 1913, when he and his parents moved to Bamberg, he decided to join a group of gliding enthusiasts there. Led by government architect Friedrich Harth, the group carried out flying experiments with homemade gliders on the Ludwager Kulm. As the terrain did not suit their growing requirements however, in the spring of the following year Harth moved their experiments to the Heidelstein in the Rhön, where he also built an aircraft shed. There Harth and Messerschmitt worked on their first combined project, the S 4 glider. The outbreak of the First World War put an end to further developments as Harth and his companions were drafted by the army. In May 1915 Willy Messerschmitt returned to continue the work of his mentor Friedrich Harth, now serving at the front, however he found that the aircraft shed on the Heidelstein had been broken into and ransacked and the S 4 glider destroyed. When Messerschmitt learned that Harth would be coming home on leave in 1917, he began building a new glider from the usable remnants of the S 4 with the aid of Harth's remaining drawings and directions sent by letter. The result was the "S 5 Harth-Messerschmitt Type Wing-Controlled Glider" (pivoting wing). The next year he produced another glider, the S 6, and after the war Harth and Messerschmitt resumed their work on the Heidelstein. In 1918 and 1920 they produced two more gliders, the S 7 and S 8. On 13 September 1921 the latter flew for 21 minutes in gale-force winds, setting a world record. That same year Messerschmitt ended his work on the wing-controlled, tailless S 9. The next year it was followed by the S 10, which the experts considered the most advanced glider produced by the pair. At that time Messerschmitt established his own company in Bamberg, the Messerschmitt Flugzeugbau. After the S 11, S 12 and S 13 gliders were only moderately successful, in 1923 two examples of the Messerschmitt S 14 glider successfully took part in the Rhön competition. At the end of the same year Willy Messerschmitt completed his studies at the technical college in Berlin with a degree in engineering – his thesis was a glider with a single-spar wing. Messerschmitt's newly-founded company concerned itself exclusively with the design and manufacture of light aircraft with low-powered engines, such as the S 15 and S 16a powered gliders and the S 16b two-seater. In 1926 Theodor Croneiß, founder of the Nordbayerische Verkehrsflug AG based in Fürth, turned to the Messerschmitt Flugzeugbau to design and build a single-engine passenger aircraft for feeder traffic capable of carrying a pilot and three passengers. The Nordbayerische Verkehrsflug AG subsequently issued a contract for twelve of these feeder airliners, which received the designation Messerschmitt M. 18. Messerschmitt saw this as the opportunity to turn his firm into a private limited liability

company (GmbH) and in 1927 he made the necessary application to the Bavarian government. His application was rejected because of insufficient financial resources. In return, however, it was suggested to him that he contact the Bayerische Flugzeug-Werke AG in Augsburg for a possible collaboration.

The name "Bayerische Flugzeug-Werke AG" first appeared in connection with the Gustav Otto Werke GmbH in Munich, which was liquidated during the First World War and its plant taken over by Albatros Flugzeugwerke, based in Berlin-Johannistal, in 1917. Immediately after the takeover the Albatros branch factory in Munich was renamed the Bayerische Flugzeugwerke. It subsequently produced aircraft under license but produced its own designs as well. The factory was then shut down when the war ended.

When the Udet Flugzeugbau GmbH encountered financial difficulties in 1926, a new firm was founded with the help of the Federal Transportation Ministry, the State of Bavaria and the Merck & Finck banking house, which took over the assets, the claims and the debts of the Udet Flugzeugbau GmbH. The company was named the "Bayerische Flugzeug-Werke" and moved to the facilities of the former Rumpler Flugzeugwerke GmbH in Augsburg. There the company mainly built the Udet U-12 "Flamingo", the most commercially successful aircraft designed by the former Udet company. Production of the "Flamingo" was an economic success for BFW, but one that would have to end some day. When Dipl.Ing. Messerschmitt concluded a community of interests with the Bayerische Flugzeug-Werke in 1927, in which the Messerschmitt Flugzeugbau GmbH would design new aircraft for production by BFW, it was a way out of the economic low in which the Augsburg company found itself after production of the "Flamingo" ended. The M.18, which was initially made of wood with later versions of all-metal construction, was a commercial success and was also sold abroad. It was followed by the Messerschmitt M.19, a light aircraft, and the M.20 passenger aircraft developed from the M.18. The M.20 was also commercially successful. In 1928 the Bavarian state government withdrew its capital from the Bayerische Flugzeug-Werke. The company was privatized and turned into a joint stock company (AG). The majority of shares were purchased by the Michel-Raulino

A Bf 109 E-7 of 7./JG 53 is readied for takeoff in Le Touquet.

Lt. Herbert Schramm of 7./JG 53 makes final preparations before a sortie.

Lt. Schramm of 7./JG 53 taxis his Messerschmitt Bf 109 E-7 for takeoff in preparation for another mission against England.

Messerschmitt Bf 109 Es of I./JG 27 escorting a Heinkel He 111 during a mission over North Africa.

Financial Group, while Willy Messerschmitt himself acquired 12.5% of shares. In the years 1928 to 1931 Dipl.Ing. Messerschmitt developed the M.21 biplane trainer, the M.22 twin-engine biplane bomber, the M.23 light two-seater, the M.24 single-engine passenger aircraft (the M.25 light aircraft was not built), the M.26 three-seat parasol-wing monoplane, the M.27 sports plane and the M.28 mail plane. Although several of these designs were economically successful, in 1931 the Bayerische Flugzeug-Werke found itself in a financial crisis and was taken over by Messerschmitt. Two years later the Bayerische Flugzeug-Werke AG was renamed the Bayerische Flugzeug-Werke GmbH. In the years that followed, the company's technical director Willy Messerschmitt designed more sport and passenger aircraft. In 1935 the State Aviation Ministry introduced a standardization of designations for German-built aircraft. As a result, the Bayerische Flugzeug-Werke GmbH was assigned the abbreviation "Bf" for all its future projects, It was first used with the Messerschmitt Bf 108 "Taifun", which made its maiden flight in the spring of 1934. One year later, Messerschmitt's Bf 109 V1 won a competition for a single-engine fighter, beating out competing designs from Heinkel, Arado and Focke-Wulf.

On 1 July 1938 the Bayerische Flugzeug-Werke GmbH was renamed the Messerschmitt AG and all subsequent designs bore the abbreviation "Me" instead of "Bf". In addition to the Messerschmitt AG based in Augsburg, during the Second World War there was also a Messerschmitt GmbH with headquarters in Regensburg.

The "Sniffling Raven" was the Gruppe emblem of II./JG 51 and was produced in several versions. It was also used as the Staffel emblem of 5. and 6./JG 51 and 2./JG 71.

The Predecessors of the Bf 109 E

After production of the early B and C versions of the Bf 109, which were both powered by Junkers Jumo 210 power plants delivering between 610 and 730 hp, it was soon recognized that this engine had reached the limits of its performance. For this reason the next version, the Bf 109 D, was powered by the Daimler-Benz DB 600 V12 engine, which in its A version produced 960 hp and was installed in the Messerschmitt Bf 109 D-0 pre-production series. At the turn of the year 1933-34 the Daimler-Benz engineers redesigned the DB 600 as a fuel-injected engine, achieving an improvement in performance. The initial version of the new engine, the DB 601 Aa, had a maximum output of 1,175 hp. The appearance of the new engine, which was to power the planned Bf 109 E series and on which great hopes were placed, meant that the Bf 109 D-1 was only built in small numbers and was soon released for export.

Factory-fresh Bf 109 C prior to delivery.

Messerschmitt Bf 109 B-1 in service with the "Legion Condor".

Messerschmitt Bf 109 D-1 of a fighter training school, finished in the standard scheme of dark green and black green (RLM 70/71).

Early Messerschmitt Bf 109 E-4 in Luftwaffe service still wearing the mottled dark green finish.

Members of the Hitler Youth inspect a Bf 109 C at a fighter training school.

Development of the Bf 109 E – Its Prototypes, Production Variants and Experimental Versions

Prof. Dipl.Ing. Willy Messerschmitt (left) in conversation with the manager of the Wiener Neustädter Flugzeugwerke GmbH, Direktor Ing. Rudolf Steininger, in 1943.
Photo: Wernfried Haberfellner Archive

The first prototype of the new E series was the Messerschmitt Bf 109 V15 with the Werknummer 1773 and the civil registration D-IPHR, which was converted from a Bf 109 D-0. As the Daimler-Benz DB 601 engine was larger and heavier than the Junkers Jumo 210, its installation in the prototype required a number of changes. These included structural reinforcements and redesign of the engine bearers and the water and oil cooling systems. Two radiators housed beneath the wings replaced the single unit of the Jumo engine, while the oil cooler was positioned beneath the engine. The supercharger air intake on the port side of the fuselage caused problems and various types had to be investigated and flight tested before a satisfactory shape was finally found. The new DB 601 A engine performed flawlessly during the numerous flight tests. It did, however, have a somewhat higher rate of fuel consumption than the Jumo 210, and the previous 337-liter fuel tank was replaced by a 400-liter unit. The aircraft's increased weight also made necessary a strengthened undercarriage. The Bf 109 V15 was also fitted with a three-blade variable-pitch VDM propeller with a diameter of 3.10 meters. Test pilot Dr. Hermann Wurster began flight trials on 18 December 1937. On 4 February 1938 the V15, now wearing the aircraft code CE+BF, arrived at the Rechlin Proving Station for performance evaluation tests. The second prototype, the Bf 109 V15a (Werk-Nr. 1774, D-ITPD), began testing on 21 April 1938. On 7 June 1938, after the completion of flight trials during which several modifications were made to the Daimler-Benz engine, the Bf 109 V15a also went to Rechlin for final evaluation. The more powerful Daimler-Benz DB 601 A engine gave both prototypes a maximum speed that was about 100 kph higher than that of the earlier versions, however the DB 601's higher fuel consumption resulted in reduced range. The increased weight of both aircraft also resulted in a higher wing loading, and for the same reason the number of undercarriage failures rose. According to older sources, the Bf 109 V14 with the registration D-ISLU was also used in E-series trials. The Messerschmitt Bf 109 E was the first variant of this fighter aircraft to be built in quantity.

After its flight trials ended, the V15 became the test-bed for the Bf 109 T with an increased wingspan of 11.08 meters and a 1,175-hp DB 601 N engine. The T was a carrier-based fighter that was to have operated from the two aircraft carriers envisaged in the Kriegsmarine's Z Plan. Of the two ships, only the first, the "Graf Zeppelin", was laid down in Kiel on 8 December 1938. Technical problems delayed construction and changing priorities after the outbreak of war resulted in work being abandoned in 1943.

Messerschmitt Bf 109 E-0, E-1, E-1/B and E-1/S

The first ten Messerschmitt Bf 109 E-0 preproduction aircraft, with the Werknummer 1781 to 1790, were delivered in the second half of 1938. These ten Bf 109 E-0s, which carried no armament, were used in endurance trials with the DB 601 A engine. After these trials were completed, the first Emils were sent to the fighter training school in Werneuchen. During its test phase, the Bf 109 E-0 with the Werknummer 1781 and the civil registration D-IECY was briefly sent to Rechlin for performance evaluations. Fourteen examples of the first production version, the Bf 109 E-1, subsequently appeared, bearing the Werknummer 1791 to 1804. The first two aircraft, 1791 and 1792, were completed by the Bayerische Flugzeug Werke in Augsburg in November 1938. The remaining eleven E-1s of the first production batch, on the other hand, were built under license. Werknummer 1791 with the registration D-IQCP served as the prototype for the E-1 series and was used primarily to evaluate flight characteristics. Then in August 1941 the aircraft was sent to Rechlin for further tests. The Bf 109 E-1 with the Werknummer 1792, which initially bore the civil registration D-IQCP and later the Luftwaffe marking CE+BK, was destroyed in an accident on 9 August 1940. Prior to that both Bf 109 E-1s, which were fitted with the FuG VIIa radio system, were used in numerous trials – including experiments with new leading edge slats and a lengthened tailwheel. The armament of the Bf 109 E-1 consisted of four Rheinmetall MG 17 7.92-mm machine-guns, two in the fuselage in front of the cockpit and two in the wings. Each of the two fuselage-mounted MG 17s had 1,000 rounds of ammunition. Members of the Luftwaffe soon bestowed the nickname Emil on the new version of the Bf 109. This spread quickly and was used everywhere. The first sub-variant of the Bf 109 E-1 was the Bf 109 E-1/B, a fighter-bomber capable of carrying up to 500 kg of bombs on racks under the fuselage or wings. Typical loads included one SC 500, one SC 250, four SC 50 high-explosive bombs, or 96 SD-2 fragmentation bombs in a special carrier. The designation Bf 109 E-1/S was only used internally and referred to a life raft which could be carried by the aircraft. It is uncertain whether this variant actually saw service. The Bf 109 E-1 was built under license by Gerhard Fieseler Flugzeugbau GmbH, the Ago Flugzeugwerke GmbH and

Messerschmitt Bf 109 E-1s built by WNF prior to acceptance by the Luftwaffe. **Photo: Wernfried Haberfellner Archive**

the Arado Flugzeugwerke GmbH. The Bayerische Flugzeug Werke, on the other hand, did not participate in construction of this version. When production of the Bf 109 E-1 began, deliveries of engines could not keep pace with the production of airframes, and the licensed manufacturers initially stockpiled E-1 airframes waiting for power plants. This problem was soon solved and in September of the first year of the war the frontline Staffeln received 108 Messerschmitt Bf 109 E-1s, followed by 102 in October, 117 in November and 122 in December 1939.

Messerschmitt Bf 109 E-2

This variant was the first Messerschmitt Bf 109 developed and manufactured by the Wiener Neustädter Flugzeugwerke GmbH (WNF). The first Bf 109 E-2 bearing the company code WNF.1 rolled out of the factory hangar in March 1939 and immediately began flight testing. Like the Bf 109 E-1/B, the Bf 109 E-2 was envisioned as a fighter-bomber. It was the first Bf 109 to be armed with an engine-mounted MG FF/M 20-mm cannon with 200 rounds firing through a hollow spinner. Installation of the MG FF/M reduced the amount of ammunition for the two fuselage-mounted MG 17s from 1,000 to 500 rounds each. As well, the two wing-mounted MG 17s were replaced by two 20-mm MG FF cannon – a license-built version of the Oerlikon-Bekker cannon – with 60-round drum magazines. Although the MG FF was already obsolescent when the war began, it remained in service with the Luftwaffe until 1945. As the thin wing of the Bf 109 E-2 could not accommodate the magazines for the MG FFs, a bulge was installed on the underside of the wing. Tests with the Bf 109 E-2 revealed significant problems with the 20-mm engine cannon. These were never satisfactorily resolved – even in subsequent versions of the Bf 109 E – which may have been why the Bf 109 E-2 never entered production. Like all other versions of the Emil, the Bf 109 E-2's standard equipment included a FuG VII radio. Only aircraft equipped with the U3 equipment set had the FuG 17 VHF radio.

Messerschmitt Bf 109 E-3, E-3a and E-3/B

The next version was the Messerschmitt Bf 109 E-3, which appeared in spring 1939. It initially retained the armament of the Bf 109 E-2, but the inherent problems of the MG FF/M as an engine-mounted weapon resulted in it being dropped from production. Some Bf 109 E-3s were thus delivered with three 20-mm cannon and others with just two. The prototype of the Bf 109 E-3 was a converted Bf 109 E-1 with the civil registration D-IRRT, which was later replaced by the Luftwaffe code CE+BL. Older sources also state that the Bf 109 V16 with the civil registration D-IPGS was also used. In addition to large-scale production for the Luftwaffe, the Bf 109 E-3 was also offered for export as the E-3a. The fighter-bomber version of the series was logically designated Bf 109 E-3/B and was equipped with the same bomb-dropping equipment as the E-1/B. It should be borne in mind that, after conversion, earlier versions of the Emil were given later designations. That means that an E-1 could be brought up to E-3 standard or an E-3 brought up to E-7 standard and thus designated. The Bayerische Flugzeug Werke AG, the Messerschmitt GmbH in Regensburg, the Erla Maschinenwerk GmbH and the Wiener Neustädter Flugzeugwerke GmbH all took part in the Bf 109 E-3 production program. During the first months of the program WNF produced the Bf 109 E-3 piecemeal. Quantity production in Wiener-Neustadt only began in autumn of the same year, and that same winter the Bf 109 E-3 began replacing the earlier E-1 in the frontline Staffeln.

Messerschmitt Bf 109 E-4, E-4/B and E-4/N

The next variant, the Messerschmitt Bf 109 E-4, which appeared in early 1940, received a modified cockpit canopy and windscreen and armor plate was mounted behind the pilot. The Bf 109 E-4 was also delivered with and without the MG FF/M engine-mounted cannon. A fighter-bomber version of the E-4 was also built and was designated the E-4/B. A second variant was the E-4/N, which differed in having a Daimler-Benz DB 601 N power plant. While power for takeoff was almost the same as that of the DB 601 A installed in the Bf 109 E-4, the N engine delivered better performance at altitude. On the other hand the DB 601 N required higher-grade 100 octane aviation gasoline. There was also a fighter-bomber version of the Bf 109 E-4/N which bore the designation E-4/NB. The Messerschmitt Bf 109 E-4 was built by the Messerschmitt GmbH and under license by Erla Maschinenwerk GmbH, WNF and by Arado Flugzeugwerke GmbH.

Messerschmitt Bf 109 E-5 und E-6/N

The following Bf 109 E-5 was a tactical reconnaissance aircraft which was equipped with the standard Daimler-Benz DB 601 A power plant and a Rb 21/18 camera. The wing-mounted cannon were removed. Because of limited space, the FuG VII radio equipment was also deleted to make room for the camera equipment. The Bf 109 E-6/N was another photo reconnaissance variant which was identical to the E-5 apart from its power plant, the more powerful DB 601 N. In contrast to the E-5, the pilot of the E-6/N had a motorized hand-held camera in the cockpit, which was expected to deliver better results than the rigidly-mounted Rb 21/18 of the pervious model. This expectation is rather curious given the cramped conditions in the Bf 109's cockpit.

Messerschmitt Bf 109 E-7, E-7/N und E-7/Z

While the first fighter-bomber versions of the Bf 109 E were in production, thought was given to equipping the aircraft with an external 300-liter tank instead of bombs in order to improve the type's limited range. The Bf 109 V26 (Werknummer 1361, CA+NK) was selected as the test platform. The aircraft simultaneously served as the prototype for the Bf 109 E-7 and E-8. The Messerschmitt Bf 109 E-7 was originally conceived as a fighter-bomber and its ETC 500 rack beneath the fuselage could carry a 500-kg bomb load or a 300-liter fuel tank.

Because of its ability to carry either fuel or bombs, the Bf 109 E-7 could be used in either the fighter or Jabo (fighter-bomber) role. When the Bf 109 E-7 was used as an extended-range fighter aircraft, an auxiliary oil tank was attached to the port side of the engine by means of tension bands. With a capacity of 9 liters, this tank was needed to compensate for the increased oil consumption during longer missions. Otherwise the Bf 109 E-7 was largely similar to the earlier E-4, although the wing armament was "slimmed down" again to two MG 17 machine-guns. There was also a sub-variant of the Bf 109 E-7 with the Daimler-Benz DB 601 N engine, which was designated the Bf 109 E-7/N. The E-7/Z version differed in having the GM-1 "Mona" device installed. This increased the DB 601 N's performance above maximum boost altitude by injecting oxygen. After initial trials with the system in the winter of 1939-40 it quickly became service-ready. With the GM-1 system the DB 601 engine's performance was boosted by 250 to 280 hp at an altitude of 8000 meters, which increased the Bf 109 E-7/Z's maximum speed by about 100 kph for a brief period. In this case the letter "Z" stood for "Zusatzgerät" (accessory device).

Messerschmitt Bf 109 E-8

The Messerschmitt Bf 109 E-8 was a pure fighter aircraft with two 20-mm MG FF/M cannon in the wings and a 300-liter external fuel tank for increased range. The Bf 109 E-8 was powered by the proven Daimler-Benz DB 601 A engine and like the Bf 109 E-7 was equipped with the Revi C/12d reflector gunsight made by Carl Zeiss. This version was built in limited numbers by the Gerhard Fieseler Flugzeugbau GmbH and Arado Flugzeugwerke GmbH.

Messerschmitt Bf 109 E-9

The following Bf 109 E-9 was the last version of the E series to be built and was a photo reconnaissance aircraft fitted with a Rb 50/30 camera. The E-9 could also carry a 300-liter external fuel tank and was likewise produced in limited numbers.

Altogether more than 3,450 Bf 109 Es of all variants left the production shops.

Messerschmitt Bf 109 V 24

Despite various technical improvements, such as the Daimler-Benz DB 601 N engine and the GM-1 system, it became increasingly obvious that the E series had reached the limits of its performance and that a fundamentally redesigned version of the Bf 109 was required. An initial forerunner of this higher-performance aircraft was the Bf 109 V24 with the code VK+AB and Werknummer 5604. The V24 was the prototype for the new F series and was equipped with a Daimler-Benz DB 601 E engine producing 1,350 hp. The Bf 109 V24 had a new engine cowling and a different radiators but retained the wing of the Bf 109 E. It took off on its first flight on 10 July 1940. Quantity production of the Bf 109 F began in the summer of 1940, but progress was such that the first Bf 109 F-1s did not reach the operational units until autumn of the same year. Compared to the Bf 109 E, the Friedrich was significantly improved aerodynamically and its subsequent variants had more powerful engines.

Several modifications were available for the Bf 109 E which could also be installed in the field. One example was the installation of a sand filter on the engine's supercharger air intake, which resulted in the addition of the suffix "Trop" - e.g. Bf 109 E-4/Trop. Bf 109 Es sent to North Africa were provided with special emergency equipment for crash-landings in the desert. The following Umbausätze or conversion kits existed for the Bf 109 E, however they did not appear until late in the type's service life:

U1 – armored radiators

U2 – self-sealing fuel tank and additional armor for low-level attacks

U3 – installation of two Rb 12.5/7x9 cameras and a FuG 17 VHF radio

In 1941 one Messerschmitt Bf 109 E was tested with a circular oil cooler which was fitted between a propeller spinner similar to that of the Bf 109 F and the forward edge of the engine cowling. According to reports, this Emil was painted in a light finish and for a time served with Fighter School 2.

The Messerschmitt Bf 109 V14 wearing the civil registration D-IRTT, photographed in the summer of 1938.

The Messerschmitt Bf 109 E-8 with Ski Undercarriage

In the winter of 1941-42 a Messerschmitt Bf 109 E-8 was experimentally fitted with a fixed streamlined ski undercarriage, while the tailwheel was replaced by a small skid. This ski undercarriage could also be mounted on a three-wheeled, jettisonable takeoff trolley. During the winter of 1941-42 a series of takeoffs was made with and without the takeoff trolley. The Bf 109 E-8 encountered problems taking off from hard-frozen snow surfaces. As well, because of its drag and weight the fixed undercarriage reduced the speed and maneuverability of the Bf 109 E-8. As it turned out, the projects disadvantages outweighed its advantages and development was dropped in the spring of 1942.

Die Messerschmitt Bf 109 E-4 with Overwing Fuel Tanks

In the years from 1941 to 1943, the Bf 109 E was used for a variety of experiments, some of which were based on very unconventional ideas. In 1942 one such project, dubbed "Wurzelsepp", saw the Graf Zeppelin Research Institute mount two 300-liter slipper tanks on the wings of a Bf 109 E-4. The tanks were conceived to extend the aircraft's range during ferry flights. After the fuel had been consumed the tanks would be jettisoned. Although the tanks had no negative effects on the Emil's flight characteristics and various jettisoning tests were successful, the project never reached the production stage.

Die Messerschmitt Bf 109 E with Personnel Carriers

Based on the overwing slipper tank idea, in 1942 Dipl.Ing. Isermann in Riut near Stuttgart devised a personnel carrier which could also be mounted on the upper surfaces of the Bf 109 E's wings. Potential uses of the carriers included dropping agents from low level and evacuating wounded. Each of the carriers had space for one man with a parachute. In the beginning these carriers suffered from aerodynamic problems, however these were ultimately solved. It is quite possible that the same Bf 109 E-4 used in the trials with slipper tanks was also used as the test aircraft in experiments with the personnel carriers. The trials were conducted in 1943 and revealed that the Emil with personnel carriers was only 21 kph slower than without them. These trials were later continued with other aircraft, including a two-seat Bf 109 G-12, but ultimately they were abandoned.

The Messerschmitt Bf 109 E-3 as Part of a Mistel Combination

After experiments with the so-called "rigid tow" were concluded, the Luftwaffe wanted to find a method that would enable two aircraft with very different flight speeds to be operated in tandem. By the middle of the war, with the threat from enemy fighters – even over German territory – the relatively slow He 111 was no longer an ideal glider tug. Because of its relatively small size and robustness, the DFS 230 glider was chosen as the towed aircraft for the initial trials. After first a Klemm Kl 35 and then a Focke-Wulf Fw 56 Stösser were mounted on top of the DFS 230, it was ultimately decided to use a Bf 109 E-3 as the tow plane. Unlike its two predecessors, this had a retractable undercarriage, and the Bf 109 was mounted on the glider by means of connecting struts. The Kl 35 and Fw 56 lacked the power to take off with the DFS 230, consequently these Mistel combinations were towed aloft by a Ju 52/3m. For the Bf 109 E, however, taking off with the glider was no problem. After the Mistel combination had climbed to altitude on its own power, the two machines could separate in the air and land separately. The combination could easily be controlled from the DFS 230 and there were also plans to control the combination by means of a potentiometer on the Emil's stick, so that the glider could be towed unmanned. In the years that followed, these experiments led to Mistel combinations with Junkers Ju 88s and Focke-Wulf Fw 190s which were successfully used in combat.

Messerschmitt Bf 109 V26, which was assigned the aircraft code CA+NK.

Technical Description of the Bf 109 E

Engine

The redesign of the Daimler-Benz DB 600 began at the turn of the year 1933-34. Designed in 1932, this power plant was conceived as a 12-cylinder liquid-cooled inverted-V engine and was produced in several versions delivering between 800 and 1,050 hp. Developed from this power plant, the DB 601 introduced fuel injection and a supercharger and was delivered in two versions – the DB 601 Aa and the DB 601 Ba. Both power plants delivered 1,175 hp and differed only in the gearing of the propeller. The DB 601 Aa, which was installed in every Bf 109 E, had a transmission gearing of 1:0.645, while that of the DB 601 Ba was 1:0.532.

Fuselage

The outstanding feature of the Messerschmitt Bf 109 E was its monocoque construction. The individual fuselage sections were joined together on special clamping jigs, drilled and subsequently riveted together. Five longitudinal profiles were riveted together to make a fuselage half shell. The two fuselage shells were subsequently joined at the top and bottom by joint profiles and frame splices. Of plain sheet construction, the forward fuselage was joined with the riveted rear fuselage. On the left side of the fuselage there was an opening providing access to the radio equipment, pilot's oxygen bottles and compressed air bottles for the guns.

One of the two Messerschmitt Bf 109 E-1s completed by the Bayerische Flugzeugwerke AG in Augsburg is rolled out of the hangar in late 1938.

The Messerschmitt Bf 109 E-2 was developed by the Wiener Neustädter Flugzeugwerke GmbH and was the first variant equipped with an engine-mounted 20-mm MG FF/M firing through the propeller spinner. Photo: Wernfried Haberfellner Archive

In Factory 1, WNF's Subject 31 sits in front of the firing tunnel where the guns of Bf 109 Es built in the factory were adjusted. Photo: Wernfried Haberfellner Archive

Wings

The single-spar wing of the Messerschmitt Bf 109 E was of all-metal construction and its metal skinning absorbed the bending and flexing forces. The spar was a web girder with a double T profile. The upper and lower webs were attached by Dural brackets riveted on both sides, and the spar attachment fittings were also riveted to the upper and lower belts. A U-shaped auxiliary spar was fitted in the rear part of the wing, and the wing ribs were riveted to both the main and secondary spars. The skinning was plated Dural sheet which was riveted to the main and secondary spars and the ribs. The leading edge of the wing was reinforced by a profile riveted from the inside. To accommodate the retractable undercarriage, each wing had in its underside a strut channel terminating in a wheel well. All fittings in the wings were accessible by means of equipment openings closed by hatches and covers.

Empennage

The empennage of the Messerschmitt Bf 109 E consisted of a braced horizontal tail, was of monocoque construction with plated Dural skinning and had a tailplane and a split elevator. The framework of the two-part elevator was also made of Dural and covered with fabric. The vertical tail of the Bf 109 E consisted of the fin and rudder. The fin consisted of two Dural half shells and ended in a fin cap. The rudder was also made of Dural and covered with fabric. The rudder seam was covered by zigzag tape that was glued in place. The Emil's fin was offset to compensate for propeller torque.

This Bf 109 E is sitting on at the Wiener Neustädter Flugzeugwerke GmbH's compass swing platform in Wiener Neustadt. Photo: Wernfried Haberfellner Archive

This Bf 109 E built by WNF has also not yet received its camouflage finish. Photo: Wernfried Haberfellner Archive

Sylvester Wanneck, probably Wiener Neustädter Flugzeugwerke GmbH's best-known test pilot, in the cockpit of a Bf 109 E.
Photo: Wernfried Haberfellner Archive

Minor accidents were common during the test-flying of Bf 109s by WNF. The Bf 109 E-3 in our photo nears the Werknummer 5199 and the code BA+FG.
Photo: Wernfried Haberfellner Archive

This Messerschmitt Bf 109 E-7 on WNF's company airfield in Wiener Neustadt, waiting to be test flown.
Photo: Wernfried Haberfellner Archive

A Bf 109 E-7 built by the Wiener Neustädter Flugzeugwerke GmbH, still without markings.
Photo: Wernfried Haberfellner Archive

Specification

	Messerschmitt Bf 109 E-1	Messerschmitt Bf 109 E-3	Messerschmitt Bf 109 E-4	Messerschmitt Bf 109 E-7
Power Plant:	Daimler-Benz DB 601 A 12 cylinder inverted-V engine	Daimler-Benz DB 601 A-1 12 cylinder inverted-V engine	Daimler-Benz DB 601 A 12 cylinder inverted-V engine	Daimler-Benz DB 601 N 12 cylinder inverted-V engine
Power Output:	1100 hp	1175 hp	1150 hp	1200 hp
Wingspan:	9,87 m	9,87 m	9,87 m	9,87 m
Length:	8,64 m	8,64 m	8,64 m	8,64 m
Height:	3,40 m	3,40 m	3,40 m	3,40 m
Wing area:	16,40 m^2	16,40 m^2	16,40 m^2	16,40 m^2
Wing loading:		159,00 kg/m^2		
Max. takeoff weight:	—	—	—	2767 kg
Empty weight:	—	1865 kg	—	2014 kg
Gross weight:	2200 kg	2608 kg	2505 kg	—
Max. Altitude:	8150 m	10.300 m	11.000 m	11.125 m
Service ceiling:	—	17,83 m/sec.	—	16,75 m/sec.
Climbing time to				
1.000 m:	—	1 min. 06 sec.	—	—
3.000 m:	—	3 min. 00 sec.	—	—
5.000 m:	—	6 min. 12 sec.	—	—
9.000 m:	—	16 min. 00 sec.	—	—
Maximum speed:				
at ground level	—	460 km/h	—	—
in 2000 m:	—	500 km/h	—	—
in 3750 m	—	—	575 km/h	578 km/h
in 4000 m	470 km/h	570 km/h	—	
in 5000 m:	555 km/h	—	—	—
in 7000 m:	—	550 km/h	—	—
Maximum cruising speed : at 4.000 m	—	483 km/h	—	—
Range:	ca. 600 km	660 km	665 km	665 km
Armament:				
Fuselage	2 x 7.92 mm MG 17 with 500 rounds per gun	2 x 7.92 mm MG 17 with 1,000 rounds per gun	2 x 7.92 mm MG 17 with 1.000 rounds per gun	2 x 7.92 mm MG 17 with 500 rounds per gun
Wings	2 x 20,0 mm MG FF with 60 rounds per gun	2 x 20 mm MG FF with 60 rounds per gun	2 x 20 mm MG FF with 1.000 rounds per gun	2 x 7.92 mm MG 17 with 1,000 round per gun
or				
Fuselage nose		2 x 7.92 mm MG 17 with 500 rounds per gun	2 x 7.92 mm MG 17 with 500 rounds per gun	
Wings		2 x 20,0 mm MG FF with 60 rounds per gun 1 x 20 mm MG FFM with 200 rounds per gun, firing through the hollow spinner	2 x 20 mm MG FF with 69 rounds per gun 1 x 20 mm MG FFM with 200 rounds per gun, firing through the hollow spinner	

More than 200 Bf 109 E-3s were built by the Messerschmitt GmbH in Regensburg. Photo: Hans-Jürgen Becker Archive

▸ To extend the aircraft's somewhat limited range, the Bf 109 E-7 could carry an 300-liter external fuel tank beneath the fuselage.

▲ In addition to a 300-liter fuel tank, the Bf 109 E-7 could also carry up to 500 kg of bombs on its external stores rack. The Bf 109 V26 coded CA+NK served as the prototype.

▸ Instead of a 500-kg bomb, which seriously degraded the aircraft's performance, the Bf 109 E-7 could also carry a 250-kg bomb on its external stores rack..

Positioning a 500-kg bomb...

... under the fuselage of a Bf 109 E-7...

... with an hydraulic bomb cart ... ... was hard, tricky work ...

... both at the factory and in the field.

With the bomb in position, one of the armorers...

... locks the ETC 500 bomb carrier.

Mechanics inspect the engine of a Bf 109 E-1 in 1940.

The Messerschmitt Bf 109 E-9, the last version of the E series, was equipped with an Rb 50/30 camera and could carry a 300-liter fuel tank beneath the fuselage. The photo shows an aircraft of 4.(H)/AufklGr 12, probably in the Mediterranean Theater.
Photo: Hans-Jürgen Becker Archive

In the winter of 1941-42 a Messerschmitt Bf 109 E-8 was tested with a ski undercarriage...

...that could be mounted on a jettisonable takeoff trolley.
Photo: Laszlo Javor Archive

In 1942 a Messerschmitt Bf 109 E-4 was experimentally fitted with two 300-liter slipper tanks on the wings.

The Messerschmitt Bf 109 E in Service with the Luftwaffe

When the Luftwaffe attacked Poland on 1 September 1939 as part of "Case White", just under three-quarters of the committed fighter units were equipped with the Messerschmitt Bf 109 E-1. Fighter strength at the start of the Polish Campaign was as follows (serviceable aircraft):

Luftflotte 1
(Gen. d. Flieger Albert Kesselring, Henningsholm, Stettin)
- I./JG 1 — 54 (54) Bf 109 E-1
- I./JG 2 — 42 Bf 109 E-1
- 10.(N)/JG 2 — 9 Bf 109 C
- I./JG 3 — 48 Bf 109 E-1
- I./JG 20 — 21 Bf 109 E-1
- I./JG 21 — 29 (28) Bf 109 C, E-1
- I.(J)/LG 2 — 39 (36) Bf 109 E-1
- 11.(N)/LG 2 — 9 Bf 109 D-1
- II./ZG 1 (JGr 101) — 36 (36) Bf 109 B, D-1

Luftflotte 4
(Gen. d. Flieger Alexander Löhr, Reichenbach, Silesia)
- I./JG 77 — 50 (43) Bf 109 E-1
- II./JG 77 — 50 (36) Bf 109 E-1
- I./JG 76 — 49 (45) Bf 109 E-1
- I./ZG 2 (JGr 102) — 44 (40) Bf 109 D-1
- I./ZG 76 — 31 Bf 109 B, C
- II./ZG 76 — 40 (39) Bf 109

Seeluftstreitkräfte Ost
(Naval Air Forces East)
(Gen.Maj. Bruch, Kiel)
- 5.(J)/TGr 186 — 12 Bf 109 C, D-1
- 6.(J)/TGr 186 — 12 Bf 109 C, D-1

The Bf 109 was also in service with the following units of Luftflotten 2 and 3 and most of the training Division, which did not take part in the Polish Campaign:

Development of the Daimler-Benz DB 601 12-cylinder inverted-V engine began at the turn of the year 1933-34.

Lehrdivision (Training Division)
- Stab/LG 2 — 3 (3) Bf 109 B, C, D-1
- 10./JG 26 — 12 (9) Bf 109 B, C, D-1

Luftflotte 2
- I./JG 26 — 48 (48) Bf 109
- II./JG 26 — 48 (44) Bf 109
- I./ZG 26 — 52 (46) Bf 109
- II./ZG 26 — 48 (47) Bf 109
- III./ZG 26 — 48 (44) Bf 109

Luftflotte 3
- I./ZG 52 — 44 (43) Bf 109
- I./JG 52 — 39 (34) Bf 109
- I./JG 53 — 51 (39) Bf 109
- II./JG 53 — 43 (41) Bf 109
- I./JG 70 — 24 (24) Bf 109
- I./JG 71 — 39 (18) Bf 109 D-1,
- I./ZG 52 — 44 (43) Bf 109

Because in delays in deliveries of the Messerschmitt Bf 110, when the war began a number of Zerstörer units were equipped with Messerschmitt Bf 109s.

First Aerial Combats by the Bf 109 E

During the Polish Campaign, which ended with the surrender of the Samodzielna Grupa Operacyjna (Independent Operational Group) on 5 October 1939, the Messerschmitt Bf 109 E fighter secured almost total air superiority. The only fighter aircraft available to the Lotnictwo Wojskowe (Polish Air Force) in sufficiently large numbers was the obsolete PZL (Panstwowe Zaklady Lotnicze) P.11c, which had first flown in 1931. While most Polish pilots flew their aircraft aggressively, most of their successes came against German multiengine aircraft. The modern Messerschmitt Bf 109 E-1, on the other hand, was superior to the obsolete P.11c in almost all respects. According to Polish sources, 20 Messerschmitt Bf 109s were claimed shot down in the five weeks of fighting. English sources state that a total of 27 Bf 109s was lost, most of them to Polish

Mechanics working on the engine of a Bf 109 E-3.

The DB 601 A engine of a Bf 109 E-4 with the Werknummer 1480.

ground fire. In the same period the Lotnictwo Wojskowe lost 114 fighters, 138 bombers and reconnaissance aircraft, and 83 transport and communications aircraft.
On 4 September 1939 a Messerschmitt Bf 109 E-1 fired on a British aircraft for the first time. Twenty-four Vickers Wellingtons of No. 9 Squadron, Royal Air Force attacked the German battleships Scharnhorst and Gneisenau lying at anchor in Brünsbüttel, and a Bf 109 E-1 of II./JG 77 succeeded in shooting down one of the bombers.

On 30 September 1930 Bf 109 E-1s of JG 53 intercepted five Fairey Battles of the RAF's No. 150 Squadron over Saarbrücken and shot down four.

The largest air battle in the west to date took place on 18 December 1939, when 24 Vickers Wellingtons of 9, 37 and 149 Squadrons, Royal Air Force attacked Jade, the Schillig roadstead and Wilhelmshaven. In response the Luftwaffe sent aloft 10.(Nacht)/JG 26 with Bf 109 Cs, II./JG 77 with Bf 109 E-1s, JGr 101 with Bf 109 Bs and I./ZG 76 with its Messerschmitt Bf 110 Cs from Jever, Nordholz and Neumünster. In the ensuing air battle twelve Wellingtons were shot down. Three more bombers crashed in friendly territory during the return flight. German losses amounted to two Bf 109s. The bitter losses suffered by the British bomber squadrons had a significant influence on subsequent operations and the future strategy of RAF Bomber Command.

With few exceptions, the first months of the Second World War – called the Phony War by the British, Drôle de Guerre by the French and Sitzkrieg by the German side – saw few major encounters in the air. The Messerschmitt Bf 109's principal opponents during these months were the Morane-Saulnier M.S. 406s of the French Armée de l'Air and the Hawker Hurricane Is of the British Advanced Striking Force (AASF), which was stationed on French soil. During this period the older Bf 109 B and C were replaced by the new Bf 109 E. From the end of 1939 the B and C versions of the Bf 109 were largely assigned to the Luftwaffe's flight training schools, while the Bf 109 D-1s were used to form several improvised night-fighter Staffeln.

Designated Case Yellow, the German invasion of Western Europe began on 10 May 1940, with attacks on the Netherlands, Belgium and France. Luftflotten 2 and 3 had available a total of 1,231 Messerschmitt Bf 109 E-1s and E-3s, of which just 73%, or 897 aircraft, were serviceable when the offensive began.

Luftflotte 2
(Gen. d. Flieger Albert Kesselring, Münster)•

StabJG 1 — 4 (4) Bf 109 E
- I./JG 1 — 46 (24) Bf 109 E
- II./JG 2 — 47 (35) Bf 109 E
- IV(N)/JG 2 — 31 (30) Bf 109 D-1
31 (13) Arado Ar 68

E
- III./JG 3 — 37 (25) Bf 109 E
- I./JG 20 — 48 (36) Bf 109 E
- I. JG/21 — 46 (34) Bf 109 E
- Stab/JG 26 — 4 (3) Bf 109 E
- I./JG 26 — 44 (35) Bf 109 E
- II./JG 26 — 47 (36) Bf 109 E
- III./JG 26 — 42 (22) Bf 109 E
- Stab/JG 27 — 4 (4) Bf 109 E
- I./JG 27 — 39 (28) Bf 109 E
- II./JG 27 — 43 (33) Bf 109 E
1 (0) Bf 109 C
- Stab/JG 51 — 4 (3) Bf 109 E
- I./JG 51 — 47 (38) Bf 109 E
- I.(J)/LG 2 — 48 (32) Bf 109 E
- II.(J)/TrGr 186 — 48 (35) Bf 109 E

Luftflotte 3
(Gen. d. Flieger Hugo Sperrle, Bad Orb)•

StabJG 2 — 4 (4) Bf 109 E
- I./JG 2 — 45 (33) Bf 109 E
- III./JG 2 — 42 (11) Bf 109 E
- I./JG 3 — 48 (38) Bf 109 E
- II./JG 51 — 42 (30) Bf 109 E
- Stab/JG 52 — 3 (3) Bf 109 E
- I./JG 52 — 46 (33) Bf 109 E
- II./JG 52 — 42 (28) Bf 109 E
- III./JG 52 — 48 (39) Bf 109 E
- Stab/JG 53 — 4 (4) Bf 109 E
- I./JG 53 — 46 (33) Bf 109 E
- II./JG 53 — 45 (37) Bf 109 E
- III./JG 53 — 44 (33) Bf 109 E
- Stab/JG 54 — 4 (4) Bf 109 E
- I./JG 54 — 42 (27) Bf 109 E
- I./JG 76 — 46 (39) Bf 109 E
- Stab/JG 77 — 4 (3) Bf 109 E
- I./JG 77 — 46 (28) Bf 109 E

The units involved in Case Yellow quickly gained air superiority everywhere and maintained it until the end of the campaign. Over the Netherlands the Messerschmitt Bf 109 E met the Fokker D.XXI, the most numerous single-seat fighter fielded by the Dutch Militaire Luchtvaart. While extremely maneuverable, it was inferior to the Emil in all other respects. Over France the Luftwaffe encountered several more, in some cases previously unknown, fighter aircraft of the Armée de l'Air.

On 8 September 1939 five Curtiss Hawk 75A fighters of GC II/4 had shot down two Bf 109 E-1s. These were the first two victories claimed by the Armée de l'Air in the Second World War. After 10 May 1940 these two types met more frequently. The Hawk 75A, an export version of the American P-36, proved more maneuverable than the Bf 109 E. In the climb the Hawk 75 could keep pace with the Emil for a short time but then fell behind. Overall the Curtiss was slower than the Bf 109 and was also inferior in the dive.

In the spring of 1940 the Morane-Saulnier M.S. 406 was the standard fighter aircraft of the Armée de l'Air and saw action in large numbers. Though maneuverable and reliable, the M.S. 406's engine was less powerful than that of the Bf 109 E and it was also heavier than its German counterpart. Apart from maneuverability, the Emil was superior in all respects. During the war in the west, French pilots flying the M.S. 406 claimed a total of 269 victories, which was due in part to the number in service, with just under 1,100 examples of the fighter having been built.

The Armée de l'Air's most modern fighter aircraft was the Dewoitine D.520, which entered quantity production In the spring of 1940. Various internal delays resulted in the type arriving at the front in insufficient numbers to influence the outcome. One month after the start of Case Yellow there were somewhat more than 300 D.520s in service. The D.520 was slower than the Bf 109 E except in the dive, where it proved at least equal if not superior to the German fighter. Like the Morane-Saulnier M.S. 406, the D.520 was simple to fly and could easily outturn an Emil. In the course of the fighting in France French pilots flying the Dewoitine D.520 claimed a total of 147 victories, of which 114 were confirmed.

The Luftwaffe lost 147 Bf 109 Es in May 1940, including aircraft in Norway. Almost 90 aircraft sustained more than 10% damage and had to be temporarily taken out of service for repairs. The following June the Luftwaffe lost 88 Emils and another 37 were damaged. Although the Wehrmacht and the Luftwaffe had achieved great success in the fighting in northern France, the ongoing losses began to make themselves felt, resulting in a slow deterioration in the number of serviceable Messerschmitts in the frontline Staffeln. As well, the Wehrmacht's rapid advance resulted in supply lines becoming dangerously overextended. Jagdgruppen sometimes had to remain on the ground for lack of fuel. In these weeks the German fighter pilots began meeting the Supermarine Spitfire I, the first enemy aircraft to prove a match for the Bf 109 E, more frequently. The German Jagdgruppen had their part in the failure at Dunkirk, where more than 300,000 British and French troops were evacuated to Great Britain. This was in part due to the losses they had sustained in the previous three weeks, which in some cases seriously reduced their operational strengths, but also to the absence of forward bases. This prevented the fighters from escorting the German bombers attacking enemy troops and ships in sufficient strength to protect them against fighters of the Royal Air Force coming from England.

The Luftwaffe began the air war against Great Britain in July 1940 with attacks on British convoys. On 1 August 1940 German chancellor Adolf Hitler issued his Directive No. 17 for "the intensified sea and air war against England", a prelude to "Operation Sea Lion", the invasion of Great Britain:

> "...the German air force, employing all the means at its disposal, is to defeat the English air force as quickly as possible ..."

Codenamed "Eagle", the intensified air war against England, now generally known as the "Battle of Britain", began on 13 August 1940. The Luftwaffe flew a total of 1,485 sorties that day, followed by 2,119 on 14 August. This was the massive opening act of the first pure aerial offensive in the history of warfare. Luftflotten 2 and 3 based in France and Belgium readied the following fighter for the battle. The variants of the Bf 109 E shown below are based on the period from August 1940 until the end of the year. The numbers in parentheses indicate serviceable aircraft.

Luftflotte 2
(GFM Albert Kesselring, Brussels)
- Stab and 3 Gruppen of JG 3
  100 (81) Bf 109 E-3, E-4
- Stab and 3 Gruppen of JG 26
  112 (88) Bf 109 E-3, E-4
- Stab and 3 Gruppen of JG 26
  97 (89) Bf 109 E-3, E-4
- Stab and 3 Gruppen of JG 52
  82 (60) Bf 109 E-3, E-4
- Stab and 3 Gruppen of JG 54
  112 (92) Bf 109 E-3, E-4
- I.(J)/LG 2 + II.(S)/LG 2
  78 (78) Bf 109 E-4, E-4/B, E-7
- EGr 210 30 (15) Bf 109 E-4/B, Bf 110

Luftflotte 3
(GFM Hugo Sperrle, Paris)
- Stab and 3 Gruppen of JG 2
  98 (74) Bf 109 E-3, E-4
- Stab and 3 Gruppen of JG 27
  122 (103) Bf 109 E-3, E-4
- Stab and 3 Gruppen of JG 53
  112 (88) Bf 109 E-3, E-4

At the start of the German aerial offensive these approximately 760 Messerschmitt Bf 109 Es faced about 1,200 British fighters, of which less than 750 were serviceable, however. In August 1940 the Royal Air Force had 67 fighter squadrons in central and southern England, of which 38 were equipped with the reliable Hawker Hurricane I. Although the Hurricane had been designed at about the same time as the Bf 109, it was a disappointment at altitudes above 6000 meters, where its speed and climb rate were inferior to those of the Emil. The Hurricane I also had a less powerful engine and its airframe produced more drag. Below 6000 meters, however, the British fighter was more maneuverable than the Bf 109 E. One big advantage of the Hurricane was its robustness, which many RAF pilots came to appreciate. The sturdy Hurricane was often able to regain its base despite severe battle damage. As more Supermarine Spitfire Is entered service in the summer and fall of 1940, the Hurricanes could increasingly be assigned to take on the German bombers, Stukas and reconnaissance aircraft. When the Battle of Britain was over, it was discovered that the Hawker Hurricane had shot down more German aircraft than all other British fighter aircraft combined. Two squadrons of the Royal Air Force were equipped with the Boulton-Paul Defiant I, whose performance was inferior to that of the Hurricane. For a brief time during the fighting in France, the single-engined, two-seat fighter had come as a nasty surprise to the German pilots, as the Defiant's armament consisted of four machine-guns in a power-operated turret behind the pilot's cockpit. If, for example, a Bf 109 attacked a Defiant, which could easily be mistaken for a Hurricane, from behind, it was greeted by a hail of .303 inch bullets from its four turret-mounted Browning machine-guns. Once the German side became aware of the aircraft's peculiarities, the Boulton-Paul Defiant I suffered heavy losses – especially in the fighting at Dunkirk. Losses were such that it could no longer be used in the fighter role. The Defiant II was later used as a night-fighter.

This DB 601 A engine is fitted with the auxiliary oil tank that was required when an auxiliary fuel tank was used.

◂ **Although they appeared in close succession, the cockpits of the Bf 109 E-7 ...**

▴ **... and Bf 109 E-8 still differed in detail.**

One squadron of RAF Fighter Command was still equipped with the Gloster Gladiator biplane fighter, which had first flown in 1934 and by 1940 was completely obsolete. Seven more RAF fighter squadrons were equipped with the Bristol Blenheim IF twin-engined fighter. The Blenheim I light bomber had entered production in 1935 and, in addition to the bomber's standard armament of one .303 machine-gun in the port wing and another in a power-operated dorsal turret, the Blenheim IF (the "F" stood for Fighter) was armed with four forward-firing Browning machine-guns of the same caliber in a ventral tray. The Blenheim I's performance was such that it had difficulty keeping pace with the German bombers and therefore posed no great threat to the Luftwaffe as a heavy fighter. As well, on a number of occasions British fighter pilots attacked Blenheims after mistaking them for Ju 88s. Ultimately this British heavy fighter shared the fate of the Boulton-Paul Defiant and was employed as a night-fighter. By far the Messerschmitt Bf 109 E's most dangerous opponent during the Battle of Britain was the new Supermarine Spitfire I, which in August 1940 made up about one-third of Fighter Command's strength with 19 squadrons. The Spitfire was England's first all-metal fighter aircraft and like the Bf 109 followed the philosophy of placing the most powerful engine available in the smallest possible airframe. The months that followed saw the beginning of a race between the two fighter types that was to last until the end of the war, with each machine taking turns "getting a nose ahead" of the other. In addition, both types were very popular with their own people. Enthusiasts began arguing – an argument that continues to this day – as to which of the two machines was the better fighter aircraft. In the summer of 1940 the two fighters were largely equal and, then as now, it was purely a matter of taste as to which aircraft was given the nod. Whereas the Supermarine Spitfire I was somewhat more maneuverable, the Messerschmitt Bf 109 E was superior in the climb below 600 meters and admittedly better in a long dive. Above 600 meters the Spitfire was superior, which the German pilots countered by diving, as the Bf 109 E could not be caught by a Spitfire I in a dive. At higher altitudes the performance of the Spitfire I dropped off again compared to the Bf 109 E. The Spitfire I's greatest disadvantage against its German counterpart, however, was the fact that its Rolls-Royce Merlin engine lacked fuel injection like the Bf 109 E's Daimler-Benz DB 601 A. This meant that, during aerial combat, the Spitfire's engine cut out under negative G, at the top of a loop for example. The Bf 109 E's fuel-injected engine prevented this from happening, providing German fighter pilots with maximum engine power in every situation. Another advantage of the Bf 109 E compared to the Spitfire I during the Battle of Britain was undoubtedly its armament of two or three 20-mm MG FF cannon plus two fuselage-mounted 7.9-mm machine-guns. Although the MG FF had a lower rate of fire than the eight .303 inch Browning machine-guns of the Spitfire I, they inflicted greater damage because of their explosive ammunition. The German MG FF also possessed a greater range than the British Browning machine-gun, which of course was very valuable in aerial combat. One serious disadvantage of the Emil, however, was its limited range. Consequently the escort fighters could spend only a limited amount of time over London. This short range of course also had a very negative effect on the German bombers, which had to attack targets located north of London, as they were forced to fly the rest of the way without fighter escort.

When the air battles over southern England began, the RAF had many more Hurricane than Spitfire squadrons (during the fighting in Poland in September 1939, for example, Fighter Command had just nine squadrons of Spitfires), and despite the Spitfire's outstanding qualities German fighter pilots flying the Bf 109 E showed themselves to be superior – after all their air combat tactics were better, having been refined during the Spanish Civil War and the fighting in Poland, the Netherlands and France. In contrast the fighter pilots of the RAF clung to outdated tactics from the 1930s and were forced to learn quickly how to match their dangerous opponent. But the British learned quickly…

Production of fighter aircraft in Great Britain was increased dramatically. Pilots from the occupied countries of Europe joined the RAF, strengthening Fighter Command. The radar system installed along the British coast proved an efficient means of detecting hostile aircraft, and Fighter Command's control system enabled it to deploy its fighter squadrons very

A row of olive green Messerschmitt Bf 109 E-3a export fighters destined for Yugoslavia.

The aft fuselage of a Bf 109 E in typical factory finish, consisting of RLM 74/75 grays with the undersides RLM 65 pale blue.

Herbert Schramm, a pilot with III./JG 53 (Ace of Spades) leaves his Messerschmitt Bf 109 E-4 after a difficult mission.

During the Battle of Britain the Bf 109 E fighters of JG 26 (Schlageter) wore yellow identification markings in addition to their standard camouflage schemes. These prominent markings were later removed.

A Messerschmitt Bf 109 E-0, identified by its lack of wing armament. The colored fuselage band with the number 16 identifies the aircraft as a training machine, in this case attached to the fighter training school in Werneuchen.

A Kette of Bf 109 E-7/Trop of JG 27 scrambles in the North African desert.

The only original Bf 109 E-4 held in Germany is in the Deutsches Museum in Munich. Here the aircraft is seen at a Mölders meet at the Luftwaffe base in Neuburg.

Messerschmitt Bf 109 E-7s of JG 27 equipped with long-range fuel tanks.

Messerschmitt Bf 109 E-1 of 2./JG 26 in typical factory-applied camouflage.

E-1
5./JG 77
Lt. Winfried Schmidt
December 1939

E-3 W.Nr. 1244
II./JG 53
Uffz. Stefan Litjens
Winter 1939

E-4
II./JG 3
Channel Front, 1940

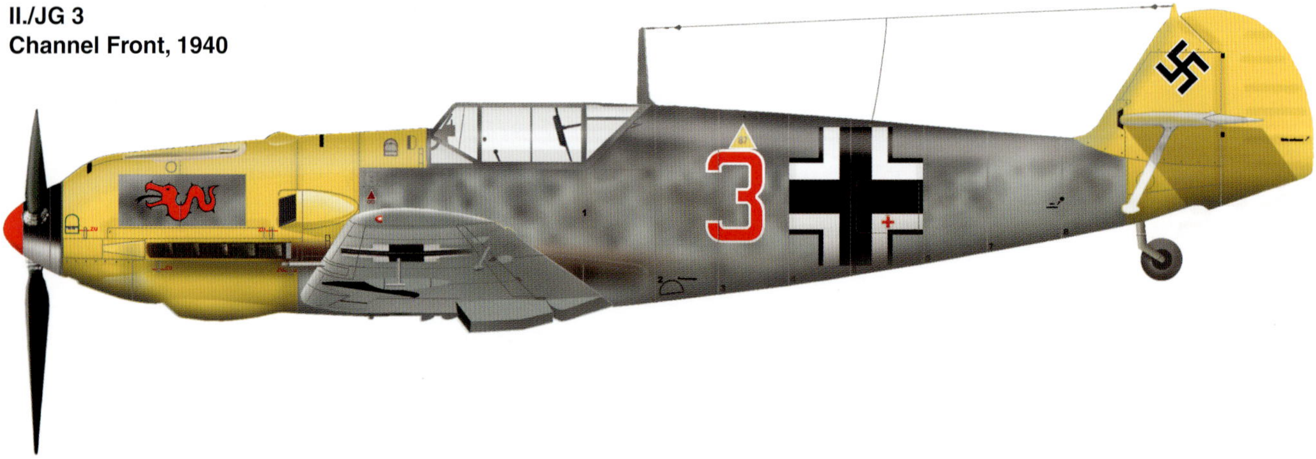

E-4/Trop
2./JG 27
Pilot unknown
North Africa, 1941

E-7B/Trop
3./JG 27
Pilot unknown
North Africa, summer 1941

E-4N/Trop
1./JG 27
Pilot unknown
North Africa, 1942

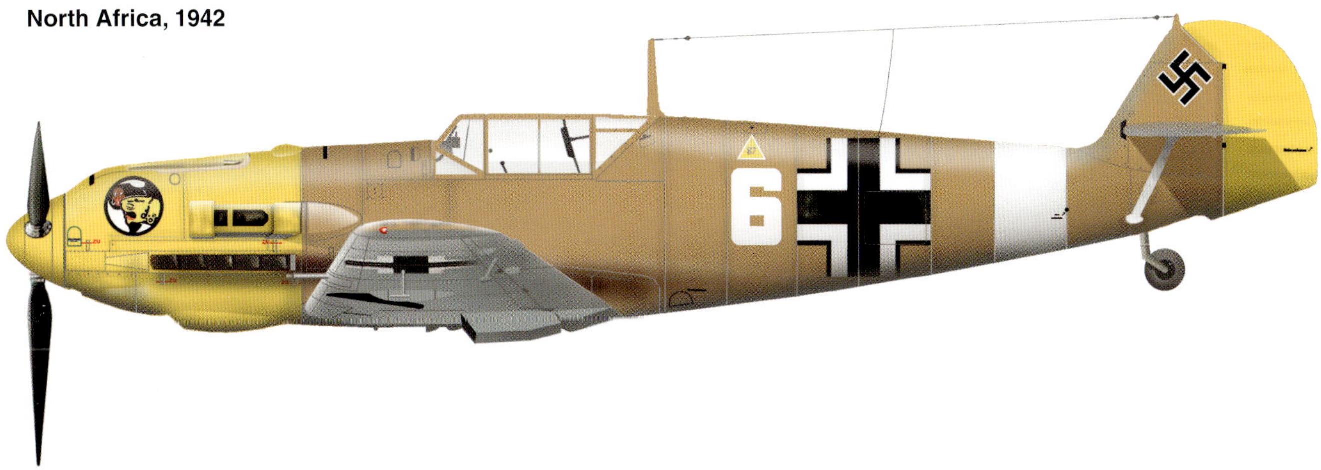

Front view of a Bf 109 E-4 during an engine run-up.

This emblem shows that this is an aircraft of II./JG 51. In the cockpit is an engine mechanic. In the Luftwaffe qualified mechanics were authorized to carry out engine run-ups.

E-4N/Trop
Stab/JG 27
Oblt. Ludwig Franzisket
North Africa, spring 1941

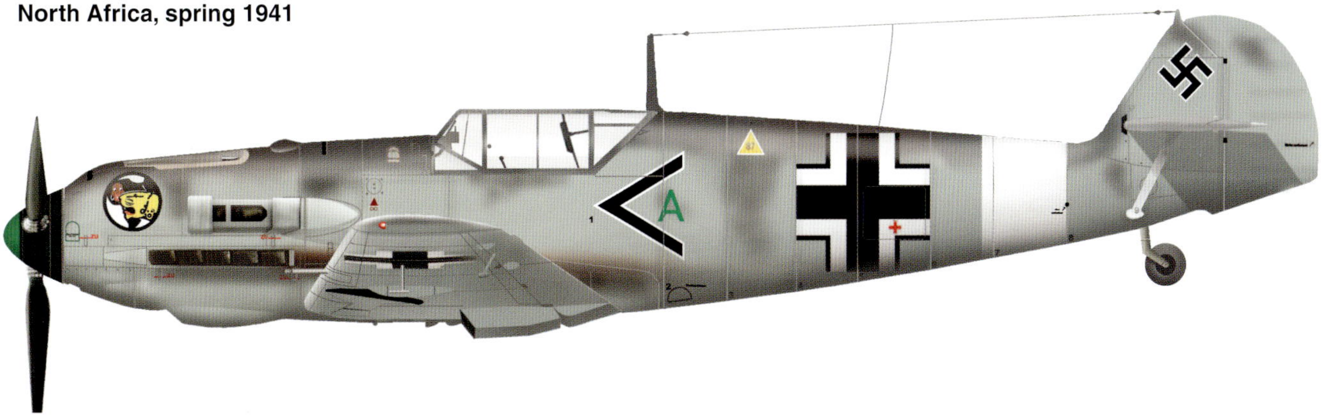

E-7/Trop
8./JG 27
Lt. Werner Schroer
North Africa, April 1941

E-7B
SKG 210

This Messerschmitt Bf 109 E-4/Trop of 2./JG 27 wears an interesting camouflage scheme (see drawings).

Lt. Werner Schroer in his Messerschmitt Bf 109 E-7/Trop over the expanses of the Mediterranean Sea.

This propaganda photo depicts very clearly the early camouflage scheme worn by a Messerschmitt Bf 109 E-1 with no mottling on the fuselage sides.

Production of fighter aircraft in Great Britain was increased dramatically. Pilots from the occupied countries of Europe joined the RAF, strengthening Fighter Command. The radar system installed along the British coast proved an efficient means of detecting hostile aircraft, and Fighter Command's control system enabled it to deploy its fighter squadrons very effectively. As the fighting went on, the Junkers Ju 87 B dive-bomber proved woefully vulnerable to fighter attack, and the Messerschmitt Bf 110 C heavy fighter, on which the German command had placed great hopes, showed itself to be inferior to the Hurricanes and Spitfires and itself often required a fighter escort. In addition, of course, there was the problem that every German aircraft that was shot down or made a forced landing in Great Britain was a total loss, which included its crew. British pilots who survived being shot down, on the other hand, were able to rejoin their units. Between 24 August and 6 September 1940, when for two weeks the Luftwaffe focused its attacks on British fighter bases, Fighter Command lost 103 pilots killed and 128 badly wounded, prompting a worried Prime Minister Winston Churchill to note: "Almost a quarter of the total of about 1,000 trained pilots have been lost." As well, 466 Spitfires and Hurricanes were destroyed or seriously damaged in the air and on the ground during those two weeks. RAF Fighter Command tried to respond to this threatening situation through tactical measures. One consequence of this was that the British fighter squadrons were no longer to attack the German formations in twos, but instead were to attack in formations of at least twenty fighters. As well, Air Vice Marshall Park, whose 11 Group in the southeast of England was bearing the brunt of the fighting, was now to be supported by 10 Group in the southwest of the island and 12 Group positioned in north-central England.

The fuselage of the Messerschmitt Bf 109 E was of monocoque construction. This photo shows the interior of the fuselage looking aft.

The empennage of the Bf 109 E was also of monocoque construction. The rudder framework was made of Dural and the rudder itself was fabric-covered.

When the Jagdgruppen, which usually positioned themselves above the bombers so as to be able to attack intercepting fighters from above, were ordered to remain at the same altitude as the bombers, which were taking heavy losses, the Messerschmitt Bf 109 Es gave up their advantage of superior speed. In the air battles that followed they were outturned by both the Spitfires and Hurricanes. The commander-in-chief of the Luftwaffe, Reichsmarschall Hermann Göring, turned a deaf ear to all arguments against this new tactic by his fighter pilots, which of course did nothing to improve their morale.

In August 1940 the Luftwaffe flew a total of 4,779 sorties against targets in England, dropping 4,447 tons of high-explosive and 1,891 tons of incendiary bombs. In the fierce air battles the Germans lost 252 Messerschmitt Bf 109 Es and 215 bombers. In return the RAF lost 359 aircraft. As the German fighter arm failed to achieve air superiority over England, however – the Luftwaffe bombers were always attacked by British fighters, suffering ever higher losses – at the end of the month Reichsmarschall Göring ordered that every Jagdgruppe of Luftflotten 2 and 3 should provide a fighter-bomber Staffel. This new tactic also had its dark side, for with a bomb beneath its fuselage the Bf 109 E of course became slow and cumbersome. If British fighters appeared before the Jabos reached their targets, the German pilots of course jettisoned their bombs so as to be able to defend themselves. The German fighter-bombers therefore failed to reach many of their targets.

This Bf 109 E-4 with the Werknummer 1480 was shot down over England on 5 September 1940. This photo offers a clear view of the two MG 17 machine-guns mounted in the upper forward fuselage.

Although the 20-mm MG FF/M engine-mounted cannon was installed in the E-2, E-3 and E-4 versions of the Bf 109, constant problems resulted in its deletion from later production aircraft of the Bf 109 E-3 and E-4 series.

Between July and October 1940 the Luftwaffe lost 1,792 aircraft over Great Britain, including 610 Bf 109 Es and 235 Bf 110 Cs. In the same period RAF Fighter Command lost 1,172 fighter aircraft, including 631 Hawker Hurricanes, 403 Supermarine Spitfires, 110 Bristol Blenheim Ifs and 23 Boulton-Paul Defiants. By autumn the air forces of both sides were seriously decimated and exhausted, without either side having been able to achieve a decisive success. The Luftwaffe's experience with the Emil during the Battle of Britain accelerated the development and production of the new Messerschmitt Bf 109 F (Friedrich).

For the Luftwaffe, the Battle of Britain ended in failure, with heavy losses, and "Operation Sea Lion" was finally called off. It had little time to recover, however, for in April 1941 it faced its next major task. After a coup in Yugoslavia on 26 March 1941 and a change in political alignment toward the Allies by the new government, the German command decided to launch "Operation Marita", the occupation of Yugoslavia and Greece. As a result of this new situation the German command saw a threat to its southern flank and access to the Rumanian oil fields, as well as to its planned attack on the Soviet Union. At the same time, the troops of Germany's ally Italy, which had marched into Greece from Albania on 28 October 1940, were being outfought by an efficient Greek army, which also had the support of Great Britain. After the Italians achieved some minor initial successes, they were forced back to Albania by the British and Greek troops and a military disaster seemed imminent.

Brand new Messerschmitt Bf 109 Es parked in front of the Wiener Neustädter Flugzeugwerke GmbH's Factory 1. Photo: Wernfried Haberfellner Archive

During the campaign against Yugoslavia, which began on 6 April 1941 and was also called the "April War", the Messerschmitt Bf 109 E-4s and E-7s of the Luftwaffe encountered hostile aircraft of their own type for the first time. In the 1920s the Kingdom of Yugoslavia had purchased Dornier D and Y and later Dornier Wal and Do 22 seaplanes. In 1937 the Vazduhoplovsto Vojske Kraljevine (Royal Yugoslavian Air Force) received 36 Dornier Do 17K bombers and on 5 April 1939 ordered 50 Messerschmitt Bf 109 E-3s plus 25 Daimler-Benz DB 601 A engines. On 23 June the order was increased from 50 to 100 Bf 109 E-3s, of which the first three were ferried to Yugoslavia in the late summer of 1939. After the outbreak of war on 1 September 1939, however, deliveries of the "mesersmitske" to Yugoslavia were held up, and of the original 100 Bf 109 E-3s ordered, just 73 were ultimately delivered. Despite the problems the Yugoslavian pilots encountered in converting to the new aircraft type, in April 1941 there were still 61 Bf 109 E-3s on hand with three Yugoslavian fighter groups. Luftflotte 4 and the VIII Fliegerkorps assembled 1,570 aircraft for the attack on Yugoslavia and the Italian Regia Aeronautica 666. The combined air forces had 1,062 bombers plus 885 fighters and 289

Brand new Messerschmitt Bf 109 Es parked in front of the Wiener Neustädter Flugzeugwerke GmbH's Factory 1.
Photo: Wernfried Haberfellner Archive

This Messerschmitt Bf 109 E-3 was photographed in Pöcking, barely 30 km southwest of Munich, at the end of January 1940.

The following series of photos of a Messerschmitt Bf 109 E-1 of III./JG 20 ...

.. depicting the arming of the aircraft...

...was taken in early 1939 for propaganda purposes.

reconnaissance aircraft. They were assembled in Bulgaria, Ostmark (the former Austria), Rumania and Hungary. Fighter protection for "Operation Marita" was provided by II./JG 54 and I./JG 27 from Graz, III./JG 54 and 4./JG 54 from Arad, Stab and III./JG 77 from Deta, and Stab, II. and III./JG 27 plus II.(S)/LG 2 from Belica, Sofia-Vrba and Sofia-Wraschdebna. All of the German fighter and fighter-bomber Staffeln were by then equipped with the Bf 109 E-4 and E-7. On 6 April 1941 the campaign in the Balkans began with the attack on the Kingdom of Yugoslavia. During the offensive German and Yugoslavian Emils of course met and there were victories and losses on both sides. During the German attacks on the capital city of Belgrade the Yugoslavian anti-aircraft guns stationed there fired at everything that came in range, endangering the Bf 109 Es of both the Luftwaffe and the Vazduhoplovsto Vojske Kraljevine Jugoslavije (VVKJ). Other Yugoslavian fighter aircraft faced by the Messerschmitt Bf 109 E-4s and E-7s included the Hawker Hurricane I ("Hoker Hariken"); the Ikarus IK-3, a Yugoslavian-developed fighter of which only a few examples had entered service; the obsolete Hawker Fury biplane; and the equally obsolete Ikarus IK-2, also designed and built

A pilot of III./JG 20 clambers into the cockpit of his Messerschmitt Bf 109 E-1 at the beginning of 1939.

in Yugoslavia. Yugoslavia surrendered on 17 April 1941. The Messerschmitt fighters of the VVKJ were constantly in action during the eleven days of fighter and claimed to have shot down seven Bf 109 E-4s and E-7s of the Luftwaffe. On the other hand the Yugoslavians lost all of their Bf 109 E-3s. The Wehrmacht captured four intact Yugoslavian Emils, which were passed on to the Soviet Union. Italian forces captured the wrecks of several Yugoslavian E-3s, one of which was made flyable again. The aircraft was not given a Regia Aeronautica registration however.

The island of Malta was used as a base from which British air and sea units could interdict supplies en route to the German Africa Corps. During the first half of 1941 the Luftwaffe's Bf 109 Es were used primarily in the fighter role during operations against the island, and in the second half of the year they were replaced by the more modern Bf 109 F. While 7./JG 26 and III./JG 27 continued to fly the Emil until June 1941, between December 1941 and May 1942 all of JG 53, II./JG 3 and I./ JG 77, all of which were deployed against Malta, converted onto the Friedrich. The same thing took place in the North African theater. Over Malta and North Africa, meanwhile, the RAF had introduced the Spitfire V, the next generation fighter that replaced the Spitfire I of the Battle of Britain. It was superior to the Emil in almost every respect. Later versions of another familiar opponent, the Hawker Hurricane, also saw service in North Africa in large numbers. In contrast to the Spitfire V however, the Hurricane was no match for

The "Black Men" prepare this Bf 109 E-1 of III./JG 20 for takeoff.

In order to extend the Bf 109 E's range, one aircraft (Bf 109 E-3) was fitted with a tow coupling in the fuselage nose. The engine-mounted cannon had to be removed. Towing experiments behind a Bf 110 proved to be too dangerous and the experiments were halted. The pilot during the towing experiments was the legendary Heini Dittmar.

A short nap on the wing of this Messerschmitt Bf 109 E-3 of 6./JG 53 was surely very restful—and the parachute is already lying on the tailplane in preparation for the next sortie.

the German fighters. The Hurricane IIA, IIB and IIC were used in a variety of roles, including ground attack and night-fighter. Other British fighters encountered in the North African theater included the obsolete Gloster Gladiator, the Fairey Fulmar I and Grumman Martlet III carrier-based fighters (the latter a version of the American Grumman F4F-3A Wildcat), the Curtiss Kittyhawk and the twin-engined Bristol Beaufighter I and Bristol Blenheim IVF, both heavy fighters. While the Beaufighter later proved an outstanding anti-shipping and ground attack aircraft, the slow Blenheim IV was a conversion of a light bomber into a night-fighter similar to the earlier Blenheim IF that saw action in the Battle of Britain. By that year the Grumman Martlet was no longer among the most modern fighter aircraft and the Fairey Fulmar was a two-seat naval fighter with no rearward-firing armament. Neither posed any serious threat to the Messerschmitt Bf 109 E or F. The Curtiss Kittyhawk that saw service in North Africa was a development of the P-36, which German pilots had encountered over France as the Curtiss Hawk 75. The Kittyhawk was widely used as a fighter-bomber in North Africa, even though its maximum speed was similar to that of the now slightly obsolescent Bf 109 E. The Kittyhawk was robust and maneuverable but its climbing performance was inferior to both versions of the Bf 109. Nevertheless, the Kittyhawk and its American counterpart the P-40 enjoyed success against German and Italian multi-engine aircraft, claiming 420 victories in North Africa.

The initial inferiority of the British fighters was of course based on technical performance data, for in the hands of a capable pilot any of these aircraft could pose a threat to either version of the Bf 109. Another serious opponent appeared in the Mediterranean skies in the spring of 1942 – the Supermarine Seafire Ib, a navalized version of the Spitfire V. At about the same time British aircraft Carriers were also equipped with the Hawker Sea Hurricane, whose performance was no better than its land-based equivalents.

"Operation Barbarossa" began on 22 June 1941 and the Luftwaffe deployed Luftflotten 1, 2, 4 and 5 for the attack. By that time the Bf 109 E's career had already passed its zenith and the majority of the Jagdgruppen committed to the operations were equipped with the Messerschmitt Bf 109 F. The Emil continued to serve as a fighter-bomber with the Luftwaffe and a fighter with the air forces of Germany's allies. The Bf 109's main opponents during the opening phase of "Operation Barbarossa" were the fighter biplanes of the Voenno Vozdushnye Sily (Russian Air Force), the Polikarpov I-15 Chato, I-152 and I-153 and the Polikarpov I-16 Rata monoplane. Some of the longer-serving German pilots had

"White 3", a Bf 109 E-1 of III./JG 20 in 1939. In November 1940 7./JG 51 took over the Staffel emblem, the "White Bow and Arrow".

This photo of a Bf 109 E-1 of II./JG 54 was probably taken before the war. The "Lion of Aspern"" Gruppe emblem was adopted from the Austrian military in 1938 and in the summer of 1940 was passed on to I./JG 76.V

already encountered the Chato and Rata during the Spanish Civil War, where they were used in large numbers by the Republicans. By the summer of 1941 both Soviet fighters were obsolete and hopelessly inferior to the Bf 109 E and F in engine power and speed, however their numbers, their maneuverability and the Soviet tactics based on these two factors made them a threat to an inattentive German fighter pilot. Despite the appearance of more modern Soviet fighter types, many German fighter pilots considered the Polikarpov I-16 the most difficult Soviet fighter to defeat in aerial combat during the war. The Mikoyan-Gurevich MiG-1 and the improved MiG-3 appeared as the Bf 109 E's career as a frontline fighter was coming to an end. The MiG-3 was a lightweight aircraft with good flight characteristics and was equal to the Bf 109 E in many respects. The more modern Bf 109 F proved superior to the MiG-3 in climb and speed, however. A contemporary of the MiG-3 in the VVS was the Lavochkin-Gorbunov-Gudkov LaGG-3, which was somewhat inferior to the Bf 109 E and completely inferior to the Bf 109 F. The opinion of this fighter held by most Soviet fighter pilots is reflected in their interpretation of the abbreviation LaGG as "lakirovanny garantirovanny grob" or "varnished guaranteed coffin".

Like most of the Luftwaffe's long in the tooth aircraft types, the Bf 109 E's active career slowly came to an end beginning in the late summer of 1941. Some Emils were withdrawn from the front and assigned to Luftwaffe training schools such as Jagdfliegerschule 2 (JFS 2) in Zerbst, Jagdfliegerschule 5 in Liegecourt, France, Jagd Gruppe Ost (the former EJG 51) in Cracow and Jagd Gruppe Süd, where replacement fighter pilots could perfect their abilities on these older machines.

A Luftwaffe field workshop in 1939 with a Bf 109 E-1 undergoing repairs.

Messerschmitt Bf 109 E-1s wait for the order to take off on a mission over Poland.

The forward airfield of a Staffel of JG 53 "Pik As" equipped with the Messerschmitt Bf 109 E-3 in 1939.

The Messerschmitt Bf 109 E under Foreign Flags

Bulgaria

At the end of the 1930s the aircraft operated by the Bulgarian Air Force (Vozdusni Vojski) were all totally obsolete. In 1940, therefore, Bulgaria procured a number of training aircraft and ten Messerschmitt Bf 109 E-4s, which were given the local nickname "Strela" (Arrow). When Bulgaria joined the Tripartite Pact on 1 March 1941, its air force had 19 Messerschmitt Bf 109 E-4s and E-7s. Although the country was now an ally of the German Reich, it tried to stay out of hostilities, although it was obliged to provide the Luftwaffe with several airfields from which to launch its attack on Yugoslavia ("Operation Marita"), which began on 6 April 1941. As compensation for this concession to the Third Reich, after the campaign in the Balkans Bulgaria's armed forces were strengthened and it made major territorial gains. This active support for the Wehrmacht in its attack on the Kingdom of Yugoslavia had consequences, however. During the "April war" Vickers Wellingtons of the RAF and Dornier Do 17 Ks of the Yugoslavian air force repeatedly attacked targets in Bulgarian territory. These demonstrated that the Vozdusni Vojski incapable of defending the country against such attacks. German expectations that Bulgaria would take part in its attack on the Soviet Union on 22 June 1941 caused even greater problems. Throughout its history Bulgaria had maintained friendly relations with Russia, and the imminent conflict almost led to a revolt in Bulgaria. For this reason Bulgaria did not take part in the attack on the Soviet Union, which of course received little sympathy from her German allies. As a result of Bulgaria's stance, deliveries of German armaments fell off significantly. For example, Bulgaria only received nine more Messerschmitt Bf 109 E-7s by the turn of the year 1941-42. After American B-24 Liberator bombers from Egypt overflew Bulgarian territory to carry out the first raid on the Ploesti oil fields in Rumania, the Vozdusni Vojski received more modern Bf 109 G-2 fighters and the older Emils were gradually relinquished to the flying training schools.

Photographs of Bulgarian Bf 109 E-4s are extremely rare. This poor quality photo shows two Bf 109 E-4s during a training flight.3eine qualitativ schlechte Aufnahme zweier Bf 109 E-4 während eines Trainingsfluges.

The Staffelführer of 4./JG 53 standing in front of a Messerschmitt Bf 109 E-3 at Mannheim-Sandhofen airfield in November 1939.V

Photographed in 1939, this Messerschmitt Bf 109 E-1 of 4./JG 77 with the Werknummer 3489 was built by the Arado Flugzeugwerke GmbH.

"White 4", a Bf 109 E-3 of 4./JG 26, photographed n flight in late 1939.

In March 1940 Lt. Demes of 4./JG 77 and his Bf 109 E-4 "White 11" were stationed on the island of Sylt. Photo: Tapio Huttunen Archive

France

Beginning in the late summer of 1939, France came into possession of three Messerschmitt Bf 109 Es, all of which came down in French territory. The first Emil, "Red 3" of I./JG 54, crash-landed near Nancy on 20 September 1939. Just two months later, on 22 November 1939, Ofw. Kloimüller of 1./JG 76 became disoriented after combat with M.S.406s of GC III/7 and landed in error at the French airfield in Strassbourg-Neuhof. This undamaged Emil was subsequently evaluated at the Armée de l'Air Centre d'Essais du Matériel Aérien in Orleans-Bricy, taking part in mock combats against the Dewoitine D.520, Bloch M.B. 152 and probably the sole French Supermarine Spitfire I. In January of the following year "White 1" was sent to the Royal Aircraft Establishment in Boscombe Down, where it underwent further tests. All that is known about the

One of the three Messerschmitt Bf 109 Es tested in France. Unfortunately the quality of this photo is poor.

A Messerschmitt Bf 109 E of I./JG 27. The Gruppe emblem is prominent on the aircraft's yellow engine cowling.

The Messerschmitt Bf 109's narrow-track, delicate undercarriage was a constant problem which led to many crashes. The aircraft in the photo is a Bf 109 E-1 of 6./JG 51.

third Bf 109 E captured by the French – possibly the Bf 109 E-1 flown by Uffz. Karl Hager of I./JG 76 – is that it collided with a Morane-Saulnier M.S.406 during an evaluation flight and was destroyed.

Great Britian

The first Messerschmitt Bf 109 E to reach Great Britain, in January 1940, was the Bf 109 E-3 "White 1" of I./JG 76, which had force-landed in France on 20 September of the previous year. The following June the aircraft was assigned the RAF serial AE 479.
One of the next Emils to fall into the hands of the British was Messerschmitt Bf 109 E-4 "Yellow 10" of 6./JG 51, which was shot down over Kent on 24 August 1940 while being flown by Ofw. Fritz Beck. It was followed on 31 August 1940 by a Bf 109 E-4 of 9./JG 26 whose pilot, Oblt. Fronhöfer, also forced-landed in Kent. On the last day of the following month, Uffz. Horst Perez of 4./JG 26 belly-landed his Bf 109 E-3 "White 4" near East Dean in Sussex. On 27 November Wolfgang Teumer of II./JG 51 was shot down in Black 12" near Manston by a Spitfire. This Emil is today on display in the Battle of Britain Museum in Hendon. On 30 November 1940 Fw. Hermann Schmidt of 4./JG 53 made a forced landing near Dungeness in his Bf 109 E "White 11". Insofar as it was possible, the technicians of the Royal Air Force repaired these force-landed Bf 109 Es, which were subsequently used for test purposes.

The Bf 109 E-4, Werknummer 1480, of Oblt. Franz von Werra, adjutant in the Stab of II./JG 3 "Udet". On 5 September 1940 he was shot down by Flt.Lt. Patterson C. Hughes of No. 234 Squadron RAF flying a Supermarine Spitfire I.

The former "White 1", a Messerschmitt Bf 109 E-1, was given the serial AE 479 in Great Britain and was test-flown until January 1942. The aircraft was subsequently shipped to the USA for further flight demonstrations.

Lt. Erbo Graf von Kageneck of 3./JG 27 stationed in Graz, photographed in front of his Bf 109 E-7 in early April 1941.

Italy

During the Battle of Britain, in which the Regia Aeronautica took part with the Corpo Aereo Italiano from bases in Belgium, there were plans to equip the 20º Grupo Caccia Terrestre with Messerschmitt Bf 109 Es. Although Italian pilots and ground crew began conversion training on the German fighter at the end of 1940 the 20º Grupo Caccia Terrestre never reequipped on the Emil. During the fighting in the Balkans in April 1941 the Italians did capture several damaged Bf 109 E-3 of the Royal Yugoslavian Air Force (Jugoslovensko Kraljevsko Ratno Vazduhoplovstvo). Using parts from a number of JKRV aircraft, one of these Bf 109 E-3s was made flyable at an airfield in the Albanian capital of Tirana. Although this Messerschmitt Bf 109 E-3 was given Italian markings, it was never officially taken on strength by the Regia Aeronautica.

In the first half of 1940 I./JG 77 and its Messerschmitt Bf 109 E-4s returned to Oldendorf in Lower Saxony to rest and reequip. The "Old Shoe" emblem was used by the Stab of the I. Gruppe and at the end of 1940 was passed on to IV./JG 51.

Armed and fueled, Messerschmitt Bf 109 E-3s of II./JG 53 in the early summer of 1940 during the fighting in France.

Two fighter pilots of JG 3 talk shop in front of an Emil of the I. Gruppe in France, 1940.

Hptm. Ebbinghausen, Kommandeur of II./JG 26, in the cockpit his conspicuously marked Messerschmitt Bf 109 E.auffällig markierten Messerschmitt Bf 109 E.

In mid-August 1940 JG 27 was stationed on the English Channel. It had 122 Messerschmitt Bf 109 Es, of which 103 were serviceable.

During the fighting in France, a pilot of 3.(J)/LG 2 poses proudly in front of his Messerschmitt Bf 109 E-3. The aircraft was built by Erla Maschinenwerk GmbH.

Aircraft mechanics pose in front of "Yellow 7", a Messerschmitt Bf 109 E-3 of I./JG 52. Plainly visible on the left is the "Winged Sword" Geschwader emblem and on the right the "Wild Boar Running Uphill" emblem of the unit's I. Gruppe.

Fueling the Messerschmitt Bf 109 E of the Gruppen Adjutant of I./ JG 77.

Close-up of the Staffel emblem of 3.(J)/LG 2 on a Messerschmitt Bf 109 E-3.

Messerschmitt Bf 109 E-3 of the Japanese Air Force, above with pilot (original) and below as a 1:48 scale model.

Japan

Beginning in 1910, Japan was a regular purchaser of German aircraft, although there was an interruption when the Empire of Japan sided with the Entente Cordiale during the First World War. From 1939 to 1941 there was a regular exchange of information between the two allies and Japanese delegations frequently visited German aircraft factories. In the late 1930s the Messerschmitt Bf 109 captured the public's attention and the Japanese military also became interested in the aircraft. The various sources differ as to exactly how many Emils were delivered to Japan, however it is very likely that the Land of the Rising Sun procured between three and twelve Bf 109 E E-3 and E-7/Z aircraft in 1940 and 1941. The Japanese also acquired rights to produce the Daimler-Benz DB 601 A engine under license. After Japan entered the war on 7 December 1941, deliveries of materiel between the two countries of course ceased.

Concerning a Japanese Bf 109 E-7/Z, it is known that one such machine took part in comparative trials with captured aircraft, such as an American Curtiss P-40E and a Soviet Lavochkin LaGG-3, and the Japanese Nakajima Ki-43 Hayabusa (Oscar), Ki-44 Shoki (Tojo) and the new Kawasaki KI-61 Hien (Tony). In these trials the prototype of the Ki-61 – the first Japanese production fighter powered by the license-built Daimler-Benz DB 601 engine – proved superior to all of the other fighters, though it was less maneuverable than the Ki-43 Hayabusa. It should be mentioned, however, that the Bf 109 E-7/Z, like several of the other participants, was already obsolescent and had been replaced by the Bf 109 F in the European and North African theaters. The American intelligence service assumed that license production of the Bf 109 E was certain and assigned the aircraft the codename "Mike". When the Kawasaki

A brief rest break in front of a Bf 109 E-1 of 8./JG 2 "Richthofen" during the fighting in France in may 1940. Note the unusual camouflage finish.

The 'Yellow Dagger in the Blue Pennant" was the personal emblem of the onetime group leader of the 3./JG 2, Henning Struempel, and afterward became the symbol of that unit.

The "Yellow Dagger in the Blue Pennant" was the personal emblem of Henning Strümpel, the former Staffelführer of 3./JG 3. It subsequently became the Staffel emblem.

Ki-61 entered service in the South Pacific, many American pilots reported sightings of the Messerschmitt Bf 109 E. Later, however, the Americans were forced to concede that this was a new type of Japanese fighter, not a German fighter produced under license, and they gave the Hien the codename "Tony". The trail of the Japanese Bf 109 E subsequently disappeared, however it can be assumed with certainty that none saw action.

The Messerschmitt Bf 109 E-4 of Maj. Helmut Wick, Kommandeur of I./JG 2. There are 42 victory bars painted on the aircraft's rudder.

Yugoslavia

In addition to modern aircraft from other countries, on 5 April 1939 the Yugoslavian government placed an order for a total of 50 Bf 109 E-3s and 25 Daimler-Benz DB 601 A engines for its air force, the Vazduhoplovstvo Vojske Kraljevine Jugoslavije (VVKJ). On 23 June of the same year the order was increased by fifty more Bf 109 E-3s. Deliveries began in the late summer of 1939, when the first Emils were flown from Germany to Yugoslavia. During the months of training by the pilots of the VVKJ, some of whom were converting from the obsolete Hawker Fury biplane onto the modern Bf 109 E-3, a number of the new "mesersmitske" were lost in crashes. The number of aircraft available to the Vazduhoplovstvo Vojske Kraljevine Jugoslavije dropped steadily as a result. As a result of the political revolution in Yugoslavia on 26 March 1941 and the subsequent turn toward the Allies by the new government, just 73 of the 100 Emils ordered were actually delivered. These may have been the two main reasons why the VVKJ had just 61 serviceable Messerschmitt Bf 109 E-3s when Germany attacked Yugoslavia on 6 April 1941 – "Operation Marita". During the so-called "April war" the Yugoslavian Bf 109 E-3s flew numerous sorties, during which they encountered Bf 109 E-4s and E-7s of the Luftwaffe. When the FTG ended on 14 April 1941, the Vazduhoplovstvo Vojske Kraljevine Jugoslavije had lost all its Bf 109 E-3s – the majority of them having fallen victim to their German counterparts.

A total of 50 Bf 109 E-3s were delivered to the Yugoslavian air forces. Many were lost in crashes during training.

Side view of a Yugoslavian Messerschmitt Bf 109 E-3 bearing the code L-7.

In autumn 1940 EGr. 210 and its Bf 109 E-4/B fighter-bombers were stationed in Calais-Marck.

Rumania

Shortly before the outbreak of the Second World War the Royal Rumanian Air Force (Aeronautica Regala Romana) acquired a number of He 112 fighter aircraft. Then in 1940 an order was placed for eleven Messerschmitt Bf 109 E-3s, followed by 39 more in the following year.

When "Operation Barbarossa" began on 22 June 1941, the Aeronautica Regala Romana (ARR) still had 36 Bf 109 E-3s, of which 30 were serviceable. In the early months of the campaign the fighter pilots of the ARR in their Bf 109s were very successful against the numerically superior Soviet air force. Some of the Bf 109 E-3s were concentrated in fighter groups together with IAR 81s of the Industria Aeronautica Romano and were also used as fighter-bombers. In the months that followed, the fortunes of war turned in the Red Army's favor. On 19 and 20 November 1942 Soviet tank units approached the Karpova airfield, occupied by Rumanian units. By then just 16 Bf 109 E-3s were operational. To avoid the threat of encirclement, all flyable Emils were evacuated, after all non-vital equipment and in some cases the armor plating was removed to enable a second man to be accommodated. During the evacuation of Karpova several Bf 109s were lost to accidents or enemy fire. Soon afterwards Germany delivered 15 Messerschmitt Bf 109 Es to Rumania, however this was not enough to make good the losses. After the German defeat at

Center: Two very nice photos of Messerschmitt Bf 109 E-3s in service with the Royal Rumanian Air Force.

These Bf 109 E-7s probably belonged t I./JG 27. They were photographed during routine training.

A Bf 109 E-3 of JG 53 "Pik As" during the fighting in France in 1940. The entire Geschwader took part in "Case Yellow", the attack on the Netherlands, Belgium and France.

Stalingrad the State Aviation Ministry realized that Rumania needed greater material support and in the spring of 1943 the first Bf 109 G-2s were delivered to the Rumanians – who after June 1942 also had to more actively defend the Ploesti oil fields. The ARR's remaining Emils were either lost during the retreat from the Soviet Union or were relegated to secondary duties, such as training units. after the delivery of more modern Bf 109 G fighters.

Switzerland

The IV International Air Meet was held in Dübendorf, Switzerland from 23 July to 1 August 1937, giving the Swiss the opportunity to see first hand the advantages of the Bf 109 prototypes that took part. Despite the initial unwillingness of the commander-in-chief of the Luftwaffe, Hermann Göring, in September 1938 a sales contract was signed for ten Messerschmitt Bf 109 D-1s and 30 Bf 109 E-3s plus replacement engines and spare parts. The Messerschmitt had been selected as the Flugwaffe's new fighter, beating out the Morane-Saulnier M.S.406 and the Supermarine Spitfire. A short time later the Swiss ordered another fifty Bf 109 E-3s. The ten Bf 109 D-1s were delivered between December 1938 and January 1939 and on 7 May of the following year the first Bf 109 E-3 arrived in Switzerland. After their arrival, all of the Bf 109

Aircraft of JG 26 near Wissant late in 1940.

This Messerschmitt Bf 109 E of the first Gruppe of an unidentified Jagdgeschwader made a crash-landing on the beach of the English Channel. Photo: Miroslaw Wawrzynski Archive

Although the German command had already abandoned the invasion of England, the Luftwaffe continued its attacks on targets in Great Britain. Here Ofw. Hans Stechmann of 8./JG 3 is seen in the cockpit of his "Yellow 3", a Bf 109 E-4 with the Werknummer 5150, during preparations for another sortie.

This Messerschmitt Bf 109 E-1 flown by Oblt. Karl Fischer (W.Nr. 4851) of 7./JG 27 crashed in Windsor Great Park after misjudging an attack on two Avro Anson Is. Here it is seen being recovered by the British.

In autumn of 1940 Fw. Beese of 9./JG 26 just managed to reach the French coast in his "Yellow 11". He put his Emil down in the sand dunes near Calais.

E-3s were converted or retrofitted with Swiss equipment. Shortly before the outbreak of war – by which time 55 Bf 109 E-3s had been delivered to Switzerland – further exports were stopped. Following lengthy negotiations with the responsible German offices, deliveries finally resumed in April 1940. Swiss pilots were involved in a number of accidents during conversion onto the Emil, several with tragic consequences. Following the German invasion of France, frequent violations of Swiss air by Luftwaffe aircraft resulted in three Fliegerkompanien with a total of 18 Bf 109 E-3s being ordered to mount defensive patrols. Beginning in May 1940, there was a series of encounters between these Bf 109s and various German aircraft, often resulting in exchanges of fire. There were so many combats during 1940 that the Swiss Fliegerkompanien succeeded in shooting down a Messerschmitt Bf 110 and several He 111s in return for the loss of one of their Bf 109 E-3s. On the morning of 8 June 1940 two Messerschmitt Bf 110s shot down a C 35 reconnaissance biplane – built by the Swiss Federal Construction Works in Thun – over Swiss territory. The aircraft's crew died in the incident, increasing tensions between the two countries. A few hours later as many as 15 Bf 109 E-3s of the Flugwaffe and 28 Bf 110s of the Luftwaffe met over the Swiss border. At the end of the day the Swiss pilots claimed to have shot down four of the Zerstörer without loss. After their experiences with intruding aircraft, in early 1941 the Swiss fitted their fighter aircraft with signal rockets with which to give a clear signal to German aircraft violating Swiss airspace. In 1942 the Flugwaffe discovered that the performance

Wonderful color photo of a Messerschmitt Bf 109 E-7/Trop of Jagdgeschwader 27. The aircraft is finished in the classic Africa color scheme.

Morane-Saulnier M.S. 406 and M.S. 412 built under license in Switzerland, was below expectations. As well, the spares shortage for the surviving Bf 109 D-1s and E-3s was becoming increasingly serious. The idea of building the Bf 109 in Switzerland – for the Luftwaffe as well as the Flugwaffe – came to nothing because of strong political opposition in Switzerland. On 25 July 1942 a pair of Bf 109 F fighters landed in Switzerland by error, and the Swiss tried to exchange them for two Bf 109 E-7s. The proposal was rejected, however. With a change in the course of the war, from 1943 the majority of violations of Swiss airspace were by British and American aircraft, however the Flugwaffe was powerless against incursions by large formations and nocturnal overflights and limited itself to intercepting lone aircraft or machines that had become separated from their formations.

On 28 April 1944 a Messerschmitt Bf 110 G-4/Ry night-fighter was forced to make an emergency landing in Dübendorf. The Germans were anxious to keep the intact night-fighter, which was equipped with the latest radar and upward-firing armament still unknown to the Allies, from falling into enemy hands. Also on board the aircraft were radio codes for the coming May. A plan to dispatch a commando team was cancelled, after which the Germans initiated tough negotiations with the Swiss government for the return of the Bf 110 G-4/R7. They finally agreed that the aircraft should be destroyed in front of German witnesses. Compensation included the delivery to the Flugwaffe of twelve Messerschmitt Bf 109 G-6 and G-10/U2 fighters, of which half were extremely worn out. The entry into service of these more modern Bf 109 Gs took some of the load off the Flugwaffe's obsolescent Bf 109 E-3s, although the last Emil in Swiss service was not retired until 1948.

Erst im Juli 1942 erhielt die 13. Letky der Slovenske vzdusne zbrane zwölf Messerschmitt Bf 109 E verschiedener Varianten zugewiesen. Kurz bevor diese slowakische Staffel im Oktober/November 1942 in den Kaukasus verlegte, wurde sie in 13. (slow)/ JG 52 umbenannt. Das Foto zeigt eine Bf 109 E-4 dieser Einheit.

Slovakia

Following the annexation of Czechoslovakia by the Third Reich, Slovakia seceded and on 14 March 1939 declared its independence. Slovakia was the only nation allied with Germany in its attack on Poland on 1 September 1939, contributing 35,000 men and a number of aircraft from its air force, the Slovenske vzdusne zbrane (SVZ).

Prior to the outbreak of war Germany had held out the prospect of transferring 12 to 18 Messerschmitt Bf 109s to Slovakia, however delivery was not to take place until 1940. This promise was not kept, however, and efforts by the Slovakian government in 1940 were also futile. Not until after the invasion of the Soviet Union, when the number of Slovakian aircraft deployed on the Eastern Front dropped rapidly, did Germany take action to support its ally with military equipment. The Slovakians had to wait a little longer for the Bf 109 E, however. Not until the end of February 1942 did a group of just over 100 pilots and mechanics of the Slovenske vzdusne zbrane arrive at Karup-Grove airfield in Denmark for conversion training on the Bf 109. After initial training on the Ar 96 B followed by Bf 109 Bs and Ds being used as training aircraft, did the Slovakian pilots finally get the opportunity to fly the Emil. Training of the Slovakians on the Bf 109 E finally ended on 1 July 1942, and the newly-formed 13. Letky (13th Squadron) in Piestany became the first unit of the Slovenske vzdusne zbrane to be equipped with the Bf 109 E, receiving twelve aircraft of various sub-types. One of the aircraft was lost during its delivery flight. After further training in Slovakia, between 27 October and 4 November 1942 the 13. Letky moved to Maykop in the Caucasus. On 9 November the squadron, since renamed 13. (slow.)/JG 52, had its first encounter with aircraft of the Soviet air force. Despite their numerical inferiority, the Slovakian pilots initially did very well, even though their Bf 109 Es were obsolescent by the time the unit arrived on the Eastern Front. The success enjoyed by 13. (slow.)/JG 52 may have been the reason why the squadron was reequipped with more modern Bf 109 G-2 and G-4s at the beginning of March 1943. The SVZ's last Bf 109 Es were still in service with a "combined squadron" near Bratislava in 1944, defending the country against air attack.

In North Africa sand was a constant problem, causing many aircraft components to wear out faster than normal. In this photo the aircraft's auxiliary fuel tank is being filled.

The Messerschmitt Bf 109 Es destined for the Soviet Union were painted in a neutral finish.

Soviet Union

In 1939 a large Soviet delegation under Central Committee member I. F. Tevosian travelled to Germany and visited a number of German aircraft factories. The Soviets were shown a number of German warplanes, including the Messerschmitt Bf 109 E. After the Soviet delegation returned to its homeland, the Soviet Union placed an order for more than 100 items with a total value of about a million Reichsmark. The Soviets procured a variety of aircraft types and aero-engines. A second Soviet delegation visited Germany in February-March 1941. An order was subsequently placed for a number of aircraft, including five Messerschmitt Bf 109 E-3s. The aircraft were tested extensively in the Soviet Union – the subsequent fate of these five Emils is not known.

Spain

At the end of September 1936 several prototypes of the Bf 109 underwent operational trials with J/88 of the "Legion Condor". These were followed by examples of the Bf 109 B, C and D, and in December 1938 the first Bf 109 E-1 arrived in the country.

As the Republican Air Force was almost defeated at that time and the civil war was just about over, the pilots of J/88 had little opportunity to fully explore the new E-1's potential. The Spanish Civil War ended on 31 March 1939 and two months later the men of the "Legion Condor" returned home by sea, leaving all their Bf 109s in Spain. After the reorganization of the Spanish air force (Ejército del Aire) in July 1939, Grupo 25 had a total of 35 Bf 109 Bs and E-1s. A number of other Bf 109s were attached to the air park of the Air Force Flying School in Reus. Later the Ejército del Aire also acquired several Bf 109 E-3s. The last Spanish Bf 109 E was probably retired from service at the end of the 1940s and scrapped.

Readers wishing to learn more about this topic are advised to refer to the book Messerschmitt Bf109 unter fremden Flaggen (The Messerschmitt Bf 109 Under Foreign Flags) published by Motorbuch Verlag in October 2006.

Nice color photo of the so-called "Black Men" at work on the engine of a Messerschmitt Bf 109 E.

One of the many Messerschmitt Bf 109 Es operated by the Spanish air forces. The Messerschmitts were handed its over to the Spaniards by the "Legion Condor" when it left Spain.

Messerschmitt Bf 109 E-1 ("White 1"), which was given the code AE 479 in England. Here the aircraft is seen after its arrival in the USA, where the aircraft was test-flown by American pilots.

Closing

In closing I would like to thank Hans-Jürgen Becker, Angelo Emiliani, Wernfried Haberfellner, Tapio Huttunen, Laszlo Javor, Harry Nakano, Harold Thiele and Miroslaw Wawrzynski, who provided photographs for this monograph.

Vienna, August 2008
Rudolf Höflin

List of References

Flugzeuge die Geschichte machten – Messerschmitt Bf 109 by Hans-Jürgen Becker, Motorbuch Verlag, Stuttgart, 1996

Messerschmitt Bf 109 unter fremden Flaggen by Hans-Jürgen Becker and Rudolf Höfling, Motorbuch Verlag, Stuttgart, 2006

Flugzeuge und Hubschrauber der Luftwaffe 1933 – 1945 by Hans-Jürgen Becker and Ralf Swoboda, Motorbuch Verlag, Stuttgart, 2005

Angriffshöhe 4000 by Cajus Bekker, Moewig Verlag, Munich, 1981

Die Me 109 by Martin Caidin, Moewig Verlag, Munich, 1981

Das große Buch der Luftkämpfe by Christopher Chant, Richard Humble, John F. Davis, Donald MacIntyre and Bill Gunston, Buch und Zeit Verlags GmbH, Cologne, 1976

Aerodata Interational No. 4 Messerschmitt 109E by Peter G. Cooksley, Vintage Aviation Publications Ltd., Oxford, 1978

Twelve Days in May by Brian Cull and Bruce Lander with Hinrich Weiss, Grub Street, London, 1995

The Warplanes of the Third Reich by William Green, MacDonald and Company Ltd., London, 1972

Wiener Neustädter Flugzeugwerke Gesellschaft m.b.H. by Wernfried Haberfellner & Walter Schröder, Herbert Weishaupt Verlag, Graz, 1993

Von der Fliegerschule zum Einsatzverband by Michael Meyer and Peter Stipdonk, Flugzeug Publications GmbH, Illertissen, 1991

Die berühmten Me 109 und ihre Piloten 1939-1945 by Walter A. Musciano, Weltbild Verlag GmbH, Augsburg, 1994

Die deutsche Luftrüstung 1933-1945, 4 volumes, by Heinz J. Nowarra, Bernhard & Greafe Verlag, Coblenz, 1993

The Luftwaffe Databook by Dr. Alfred Price, Greenhill Books, London. 1997

Kriegstagebuch des OKW 1940-1945, 8 volumes, produced by Percy Schramm, Weltbild GmbH, Augsburg, 2005

Entscheidende Luftschlachten des 2. Weltkrieges by Christopher Shores, Motorbuch verlag, Stuttgart, 1988

Die Deutschen Militärflugzeuge 1919 – 1934 by Helmut Stützer, verlag E.S. Mittler & Sohn, Herford, 1984

Lexikon des Zweiten Weltkrieges by Christian Zentner, Südwest Verlag, Munich, 1977

Other Sources

September '39 by Marius Emmerling, unpublished manuscript, Wuppertal, 1994

Germany delivered a number of aircraft to Bulgaria in 1940, including ten Messerschmitt Bf 109 Es. The photo shows a pair of Emils of the 6th Polk of the Bulgarian Vojduschni Vojski in 1942.